REMADE Series

REFRESHED

REMADE Series

REFRESHED

A 6-Week Personal or Small Group Study

Michelle Rayburn

FCL
BOOKS

Refreshed: A 6-Week Personal or Small Group Study
Copyright ©2024 Michelle Rayburn
ISBN: 978-1-954576-07-0 (Print), 978-1-954576-09-4 (Ebook)

Published by Faith Creativity Life Books
fclbooks.com

Edited by Robyn Mulder – robynmulder.com
Cover and typesetting by Michelle Rayburn – missionandmedia.com
Cover image, royalty-free, Storyblocks – storyblocks.com

Books in the REMADE series:

Renewed (2023)

Refreshed (2024)

Restored (2026)

Refined

Kathy,

thank you for the deep discussions as I have processed
what God continues to remake in my life. May others
be refreshed by the fruit of your friendship.

Contents

Welcome

OVER THE COMING WEEKS, WE WILL EXPLORE what it means to be spiritually refreshed. Discover the transformative power of Jesus through a Bible study that walks you through some of the timeless stories from the book of John. Journey through life-changing encounters, including the woman at the well, Nicodemus, the woman caught in adultery, and conversations with the twelve disciples. From living water to the Bread of Life, you'll gain a practical understanding of how Jesus nurtures followers. Uncover what it means to be reborn into God's family and learn how to remain on the Vine, thriving as a branch connected to Jesus. Experience the fullness of life in Christ and the joy of being continually refreshed by his love and truth. Join us in exploring these powerful stories and embark on a path to spiritual renewal and growth. In addition to covering chapters of John in the main study every week, you'll also explore additional sections of John in the add-on studies.

WHAT TO EXPECT

I'VE SELECTED THE NEW LIVING TRANSLATION (NLT) for any Bible passages printed in this study. However, you're always welcome to use your favorite translation. I chose the NLT because it's worded in such a way that people from all backgrounds can understand. If you didn't grow up in church, you might see Scripture as difficult to understand. Perhaps you memorized verses from a Bible version that used Old English, and it's nostalgic to you.

There is nothing wrong with those translations. However, I've found that teaching from the NLT text helps us all feel more comfortable discussing and applying its principles to life.

LEADERS

If you're doing this as a group, you probably have someone designated as a leader. That's great! We all need someone to keep us on task. You might wonder why this study doesn't include a leader guide. Great question.

Think of your leader as a facilitator. Her role is to keep the discussion moving and watch for opportunities to draw everyone into the conversation. She's the sister who wants to make sure each person feels loved, valued, and heard.

Here's what she does not need to do: spend hours prepping, study the Hebrew and Greek and a stack of commentaries, and come to your group ready to teach. Whew! I heard someone breathe a sigh of relief there.

I've found that when we all come to the topic prepared to share our hearts rather than teach a lesson, there is a sweet, mutual blessing that comes from thinking together. Asking the questions and reflecting out loud. Being real and not needing to know all the things.

This study is a guide for you. I don't know *all* the things either. God's beautiful and powerful Word has an endless supply of material to study and apply. Do it together. Explore it *with* each other. And take the pressure off someone to lead.

Maybe you'll read that and raise your hand to be the next facilitator.

GROUPS AND INDIVIDUALS

If your group has more than eight participants, I encourage you to do the story part together and then cluster into smaller groups for discussion and study.

This will also provide a better space for each person to contribute to the discussion. If you make space for conversation, the shy or introverted ones have something to say—probably something profound and thoughtful.

This study can also be done online through video chat. There is no video component to worry about coordinating. With a workbook, a Bible, and a device with a camera, anyone can join in for discussion.

If you're doing the study on your own, you might consider having a friend do it simultaneously. You could chat weekly to share prayer needs with one another and talk about what you're applying that week to your life. Or you could enlist a few friends and have a Facebook group with weekly posts, an Instagram group chat, or a Discord or Slack discussion.[*]

Whether you meet in a coffee shop, church fellowship hall, living room, or virtual space, the goal is the same: growing connections around the Word of God.

---

[*] See Discord.com or Slack.com.

FORMAT

IN THIS QUICK RUN-THROUGH OF THE WEEKLY format, I'll give you some ideas for ways you can use the material. You never have to do *all* of it. If you have less than ninety minutes each week for a group meeting, or if you need extra social time when you gather, you might spread out the six lessons over twelve weeks.

There is no right way to do it. I know there is at least one perfectionist out there who needs that permission to go off script and feel free to see where the road leads. You're welcome.

FIRST THOUGHTS

This is a time of reflection before the study begins. It's solo work for you to do as you prepare your mind and heart for what God might do. Allow five to ten minutes to forget the dishes you left in the sink at home and the errand list calling to you, and just pause.

STORY

I'll start you off with a short personal story to introduce the chapter. If you're in a group, you could have someone read this aloud, have everyone read it beforehand, or take turns reading the section. This is your warm-up.

PRAYER

Have someone read it aloud to prepare your hearts for study. Or pray in your own words! It's a starting point.

EXPLORE THE WORD

This section gets into the heart of the study. Many of the Bible passages will be printed in the text. Some will have numbered verses where those are useful for discussion purposes. Having the Scripture printed will help if you all have different translations. You can read together but use your own Bible for a parallel study with footnotes and more.

The sidebars contain additional notes, Bible verses, and commentary. These are for further study if you'd like to explore more, go deeper, take a detour, spread the lesson over more than one week—any way you'd like to use them.

Again, this is designed for you to read, study, and discuss together without anyone needing to teach.

PRAYER JOURNAL

The prayer journal can be used alone, in the group, or both. I know how groups can get off track when it comes to prayer time. Our intentions are pure. They really are! But sometimes, one person talks a lot, and someone else doesn't know how to put her needs into words. Or someone else needs a moment to gather her thoughts and process them.

One way to make your prayer time more intimate is to take a moment to write in the prayer journal. Then, divide into groups of two or three people to share one thing you wrote there. You can pray specifically over these praises or requests together and even make a plan to check in once during the week with the people in your prayer cluster—perhaps by text, phone call, or email.

Look back each week and note where you saw God in action on the things you included in your prayers.

MICRO STUDIES

There are five devotional studies for you to do on your own during the week. Or, if you're doing this book solo, you might want to complete the main study one week and the micro studies the next, stretching it out over twelve weeks.

The micro studies are geared toward personal application of the main Bible study. Each one has a passage to read, a verse to write out, some application questions, and a place for you to write out a prayer that day.

HOPE IN ACTION

You'll find a variety of action steps here that connect the weekly topic with an idea you can carry out in a practical way. Primarily, they're geared toward loving and encouraging others and taking steps that help you grow in faith.

Before you begin, I'd like to pray for you:

> Thank you, God, for the person holding this book. As she studies your Word, I ask that you meet her right where she is. Open her heart to receive your love and grace in a new way. Refresh her soul, Lord. Strengthen her faith and encourage her as your Word comes alive in her heart and mind, bringing joy, healing, hope, and restoration. May your Holy Spirit guide as we trust that you will accomplish great things in and through each one who draws near to you. Amen.

WEEK ONE
REFILL

O God, you are my God; I earnestly search for you. My soul thirsts for you; my whole body longs for you in this parched and weary land where there is no water.
—Psalm 63:1

First Thoughts

TO REFRESH MEANS TO GIVE NEW ENERGY or strength to something, to update and restore or revive vitality. It also means replenishing— as in refilling a beverage cup or rehydrating our bodies. It can be literal or figurative, soul-filling or stomach-filling, resetting the button on a computer, or resetting our mindset.

What refreshes you to fullness and gives you vitality? What fills you up?

Take a few minutes to list some things that make you feel refreshed. They might be activities with people or without, things you could easily do, or things requiring a little planning. Consider what you love, even if you're in the minority in appreciating it.

STORY

HAVE YOU EVER BEEN SO THIRSTY YOU couldn't think about anything until you got a drink of water? Or were you so tired that you wanted nothing more than to collapse on a heap of pillows and sleep for a week? Maybe you've been hangry. My husband can testify that hunger, frustration, and mental exhaustion collide in my perfect storm for hanger. When he misses the exit to which I directed him, he knows what happens in that thirty miles before a sustenance stop.

My supposed starvation has been the source of many a road trip meltdown. If we're short on both food and caffeine, it's a sure firestorm where I'll verbally incinerate anyone who gets in my path. Insert eye roll here to recognize just how petty and first-world this is. I've never starved or been close to it.

If you have been around a tired child, you know they can sometimes be incredibly unreasonable when they lack refreshment. Some of our friends and spouses would collaborate to agree that adults often aren't that much better.

If you've ever been so depleted that you couldn't stand to be around another person or so thirsty you couldn't think about anything else, you also probably know how it feels to be refreshed—to quench that deep need and come back with a satisfied sigh as you wipe the drips of liquid from your face after gulping and chugging.

If the sum of your recent days includes pouring, pouring, pouring without any refilling, you need a hot minute here. Let's make that a *cool* minute.

Take a moment to close your eyes, and then take a deep breath.

How does it feel to press pause and experience a moment of refreshing? Some of you almost fell asleep there. Perhaps you—like me—have been unsure of closing your eyes during the long prayer at church out of a fear you won't have the power to open them again—where you secretly pray the pastor will keep it short or that someone will be on standby to poke you before the first snore escapes your throat. That's when we need refreshing.

SPIRITUAL REFILLING

In addition to physical needs, we have within us a deep need for spiritual renewal. Our souls need to know satisfaction and refreshment. Grace. Peace. Love. Joy. All the things that flow from tapping into God's fountain of living water.

King David wrote this prayer after committing a heavy sin and being confronted about it. "Create in me a clean heart, O God. Renew a loyal spirit within me" (Psalm 51:10).

David knew he needed a clean heart.

Do you know what *you* need? Sometimes, we live oblivious to what we really need. We look for satisfaction in so many places but can't find it. We have a continual hunger or thirst and can't put our finger on the true craving.

It's like opening the pantry and seeing boxes, cans, and bags of snacks. *Hmm. Not that.* You open the refrigerator and close it several times. *Not that either.* You head back to the pantry.

You poke around again in there, staring into the depths for a while, hoping the right thing will fall off the shelf and into your hands.

When nothing does, you close the door.

"There is nothing here to eat," you declare.

Wait, what? There are options all around. Fresh fruit, cheese, crackers, protein bars, salty, sweet, crunchy, chewy. But you don't know what you're looking for.

God often shows up before we even realize we need him. Before we ask, he approaches us—while we're cluelessly poking around in the figurative cupboards of spiritual searching. That is where we find the woman in today's story, going about her everyday life, not looking for anything but water to satisfy her physical thirst. She doesn't know how to identify her spiritual thirst until meeting Jesus.

This week, we'll focus on her need, and next week, we'll dive into how her encounter with Jesus changed her life. If you're longing for refreshment, this is where it begins—with understanding how to be filled.

PRAYER

GOD, I'M HERE WITH AN OPEN HEART, longing for your presence and guidance. I acknowledge that I often overlook my deepest spiritual needs, trying to fill my life with things that cannot truly satisfy. Show me where my heart is hungry and thirsty for more of you. I confess that I sometimes turn to quick solutions for what I really need. As I seek you, draw closer to me and transform me to desire you, above all, my provider and sustainer. Amen.

EXPLORE THE WORD

PERHAPS YOU'VE NOTICED HOW MANY CHURCHES NAME the organization after some sort of water. The River. Living Waters. River of Life. Streams of Living Waters. You've probably never seen one named Puddles of Stagnant Water, Standing Water Fellowship, or Cisterns of the Covenant. Why?

The water metaphor for naming churches comes from several places in the Bible. Jesus offered living water that would flow out of the hearts of people who believed in him (John 4:10; 7:38). Revelation talks about a river with the water of life that flows from the throne of God (22:2). Ezekiel speaks of a river that flows from the temple and waters ever-bearing fruit trees (47:12).

A river or stream paints a picture of a source that never runs out. A cistern, puddle, pond, or container will eventually dry up. But a river is ever flowing and moves with a force sustained by the source. Instead of a container that empties, it has a forever supply. Let's look at one of the places where Jesus spoke of living water.

> On the last day, the climax of the festival, Jesus stood and shouted to the crowds, "Anyone who is thirsty may come to me! Anyone who believes in me may come and drink! For the Scriptures declare, 'Rivers of living water will flow from his heart.'" (When he said "living water," he was speaking of the Spirit, who would be given to ev-

In John 7:38, Jesus said he was quoting the Scriptures about rivers of living water flowing from a person's heart. We can speculate but can't be sure exactly which Scriptures he refers to. Perhaps one of these:

For I will pour out water to quench your thirst and to irrigate your parched fields. And I will pour out my Spirit on your descendants, and my blessing on your children. (Isaiah 44:3)

With joy you will drink deeply from the fountain of salvation! (Isaiah 12:3)

The LORD will guide you continually, giving you water when you are dry and restoring your strength. You will be like a well-watered garden, like an ever-flowing spring." (Isaiah 58:11)

eryone believing in him. But the Spirit had not yet been given, because Jesus had not yet entered into his glory.)

When the crowds heard him say this, some of them declared, "Surely this man is the Prophet we've been expecting." (John 7:37–40)

Does anyone else wonder why Jesus stood up and started shouting? Does it give you this-isn't-going-to-end-well vibes? It made me wonder what I would do if someone stood up and began shouting amid a large festival crowd.

What do you think Jesus meant when he referred to "anyone who is thirsty"?

How do you think they might have reacted to an invitation to "come and drink" when he was standing there holding nothing?

A few days prior, Jesus's brothers had tried to convince him to attend the festival called the Feast of Tabernacles with them. He wanted to remain low-key and out of sight because the Jewish leaders were already plotting his death. "Leave here and go to Judea, where your followers can see your miracles! You can't become famous if you hide like this! If you can do such wonderful things, show yourself to the world!" they said (John 7:1–3).

What did Jesus's brothers misunderstand about his miracles, his purpose, and his motives?

(Continued)

I will open up rivers for them on the high plateaus. I will give them fountains of water in the valleys. I will fill the desert with pools of water. Rivers fed by springs will flow across the parched ground. (Isaiah 41:18)

"Is anyone thirsty? Come and drink—even if you have no money! Come, take your choice of wine or milk—it's all free!" (Isaiah 55:1)

They didn't get it. Isn't it just like brothers to think of his becoming famous above anything else? Jesus said he would stay in Galilee because it wasn't yet God's timing. But then, he secretly went to the festival and overheard people grumbling about him in the crowds. "Then, midway through the festival, Jesus went up to the Temple and began to teach. The people were surprised when they heard him. 'How does he know so much when he hasn't been trained?' they asked" (John 7:14–15).

And then we come to the final day of the festival, the last day of the Feast of Tabernacles. People were already beginning to believe he just might be the Messiah they had been waiting for. Some in the crowd said he was demon-possessed. But many believed because of his miracles.

But why this thing about water? The feast involved a lot of rituals and ceremonies, including the pouring of water as a symbolic act. One commentator helps us understand the cultural significance of water-pouring:

> For the first six days of the feast they used to fill a golden flagon with water from the Pool of Siloam and carry it back to the temple. When they reached the Water Gate, three blasts on the shofar (ram's horn trumpet) were sounded. When they arrived at the temple, they processed around the altar and sang the Hallel (Pss. 113–118), the people shaking their lulabs (bundles of myrtle, palm and willow bound up with a citron), while the priests shook theirs (made from willow [poplar]

The Feast of Tabernacles, or Booths, is one of Israel's three great annual festivals. This one was celebrated "at the time of the agricultural harvest, in gratitude for Yahweh's present and historical provision" after the completion of grain threshing and pressing grapes. "During this festival Israel gathered luxuriant boughs and built booths in which to live for the span of the festival. These acts were meant to remind them of the time spent wandering in the desert."*

* Benjamin M. Austin, "Booths, Feast of," in *The Lexham Bible Dictionary*, ed. John D. Barry et al. (Bellingham, WA: Lexham Press, 2016).

branches). The flagon was taken to the priest on duty at the altar who had two silver bowls, one for the water and the other for wine. These bowls were filled and then the contents poured over the altar. . . . People believed that when the Messiah came he would provide water (as he would provide manna) just as Moses had done.**

After six days of observing ceremonial pouring from containers holding limited amounts of water, Jesus stood up to say he was there to point the way to living water. He was essentially saying he was the Messiah without saying, "I am the Messiah."

This prompted a stir among the people with many of them saying, "He is the Messiah" (John 7:41).

Now that we have seen the context of this feast, what is significant about Jesus's statement?

Thirst provides a natural and universally understandable metaphor for our need for spiritual fulfillment.

A well is a reservoir for water, but when it is spring fed, it never runs dry. Describe the difference between seeing the Holy Spirit as a dynamic flow versus a static source of spiritual life.

** Colin G. Kruse, John: An Introduction and Commentary, vol. 4, Tyndale New Testament Commentaries (Downers Grove, IL: InterVarsity Press, 2003), 190–191.

How does understanding Jesus as the source of living water impact your understanding of salvation and eternal life?

How does faith connect with the concept of rivers of living water flowing from within us?

Now that we have established where the metaphor for living water connects with the Messiah and the Holy Spirit, let's hop over to John 4 to see how Jesus used the phrase with a woman he encountered at a well.

> ³ So [Jesus] left Judea and returned to Galilee.

> ⁴ He had to go through Samaria on the way. ⁵ Eventually he came to the Samaritan village of Sychar, near the field that Jacob gave to his son Joseph. ⁶ Jacob's well was there; and Jesus, tired from the long walk, sat wearily beside the well about noontime. ⁷ Soon a Samaritan woman came to draw water, and Jesus said to her, "Please give me a drink." ⁸ He was alone at the time because his disciples had gone into the village to buy some food.

> ⁹ The woman was surprised, for Jews refuse to have anything to do with Samaritans. She said to Jesus, "You are a Jew, and I am a Samaritan woman. Why are you asking me for a drink?"

Jacob's well isn't mentioned in the Old Testament, but there is a deep well in this area where Jacob owned land, according to Genesis 33:19. One New Testament scholar said, "It is a fine installation, with a cylindrical shaft seven feet in diameter and 106 feet deep driven into the rock and fresh subsoil water at the bottom (like Isaac's well in Gen. 26:19) ringed by a wall on top. There are two holes through which a bucket can be lowered [John 4:11] and the water lies near the bottom of the shaft."*

---

* Rudolf Schnackenburg as cited in Kruse, *John*, 129.

[10] Jesus replied, "If you only knew the gift God has for you and who you are speaking to, you would ask me, and I would give you living water."

[11] "But sir, you don't have a rope or a bucket," she said, "and this well is very deep. Where would you get this living water? [12] And besides, do you think you're greater than our ancestor Jacob, who gave us this well? How can you offer better water than he and his sons and his animals enjoyed?"

[13] Jesus replied, "Anyone who drinks this water will soon become thirsty again. [14] But those who drink the water I give will never be thirsty again. It becomes a fresh, bubbling spring within them, giving them eternal life."

[15] "Please, sir," the woman said, "give me this water! Then I'll never be thirsty again, and I won't have to come here to get water." (John 4:3–15)

Next week, we will return to this passage to discuss the cultural implications more. For today, consider the idea of being filled with living water. This Samaritan woman is a powerful illustration of what it means to be spiritually thirsty. Later on in this conversation with Jesus, we will see evidence that perhaps her complicated history and current living situation were symbolic of a search for fulfillment in relationships and worldly pursuits.

What are some areas in your life where you have experienced a sense of spiritual emptiness or longing?

How have you tried to satisfy that thirst in the past?

Jesus asked for something from the woman first. Based on her response in John 4:9, why was this an unusual request?

Notice how Jesus skipped the small talk. He went straight to discussing the significance of who he was and what gift he could offer her from God. Why do you think he used the word *gift* in verse 10?

The woman didn't yet realize that *Jesus* was the gift that would satisfy her. When have you not realized that Jesus himself was the gift you needed?

In the New Testament, the word used for *gift* here in John 4:10 is always used for gifts of God.[*] It has to do with something acquired or given without expecting compensation in return. It's the same word used in Acts 2:38 about the gift of the Holy Spirit.

---

* D. G. Burke, "Gift," in *The International Standard Bible Encyclopedia, Revised*, ed. Geoffrey W Bromiley (Wm. B. Eerdmans, 1979–1988), 466.

Jesus meets people at their point of need, inviting them to recognize their spiritual longing and turn to him for fulfillment. There was nothing demanding about their encounter. At first, she was thinking of literal water and how nice it would be to never have to come back to this well again.

But then, as Jesus continued revealing things about his knowledge of her life, she began to see him as a prophet who could address more than physical thirst. That quickly led into a deep spiritual discussion, which is the equivalent of if we were to have a spiritual conversation at the grocery store.

In verses 11–12, the woman demonstrated she was thinking about a rope and a bucket. Logistics. First, what Jesus was saying hadn't yet registered. And second, she was already trying to fix a logistics problem while also challenging Jesus on his credentials. Hers was a rhetorical question. "Do you think you're greater than our ancestor Jacob, who gave us this well?" she asked. One commentator said the way she asked the question in the original language indicated that she expected a negative answer. "She implied that Jesus thought too highly of himself, as if he were greater even than Jacob who gave them the well and drank from it himself together with his children and animals."*

Can you think of an experience where you didn't understand what God was trying to tell you and you questioned him?

Look at verse 14 again. "It becomes a fresh, bubbling spring within them, giving them eternal life." Bubbling up like a spring of water, which some translations call a wellspring. The woman wanted this gift, even though she still didn't understand it.

---

* Kruse, John, 131.

Have you said yes to God before you fully understood the gift he offered?

The Greek verb used for springing up here is *hallomai*, which literally means to leap or jump up.[*]

* Rick Brannan, ed., *Lexham Research Lexicon of the Greek New Testament*, Lexham Research Lexicons (Bellingham, WA: Lexham Press, 2020).

If you hesitated to answer, let me offer some reassurance. No matter how long I've had a relationship with Jesus, I still don't fully understand the gift of God's grace! The Holy Spirit satisfies our spiritual thirst and brings life. If you've lived for a long time, thinking you needed to fully understand first, here is hope. God wants to offer refilling, where your spiritual bucket never runs empty, and he keeps topping it off. Over time, that living water brings about transformation.

What specific practices or habits can you adopt to ensure that you continually draw from God's source of spiritual water?

What questions about living water and the Holy Spirit would you like to explore further?

Prayer Journal

I'M THANKFUL FOR:

_____

_____

_____

_____

_____

_____

I'M ASKING GOD FOR:

_____

_____

_____

_____

_____

_____

WORDS OF WORSHIP TO GOD:

_____

_____

_____

_____

_____

_____

APPLY

MICRO STUDY 1

Read John 1:1–28.

Write out John 1:12 here:

_____

_____

_____

_____

_____

_____

How does the idea of being a child of God through believing in Jesus affect your understanding of your identity and purpose in life? (Some translations use the words *received* or *accepted* in this verse instead of *believe*.)

Describe how understanding what it means to be a child of God affects how you see others.

In what way does receiving Jesus connect with the concept of receiving living water? Contrast this with a stagnant pond.

John 1:16 says, "From his abundance we have all received one gracious blessing after another." How does the idea of being flooded with abundant grace make you feel?

My prayer to God today is:

_____

_____

_____

_____

_____

_____

_____

MICRO STUDY 2

Read John 1:29–42.

Write out the second half of John 1:41 here:

_____

_____

_____

There are a lot of metaphors and titles in this chapter. Earlier in the chapter, Jesus was called the Word, the light, God's one and only Son, and the Lord. Here, John the Baptist referred to Jesus as the Lamb of God and the Chosen One of God. Andrew saw he was the Messiah (Christ, which also means Anointed One) and brought his brother to meet Jesus. Pause for a moment to write what it means to *you* that Jesus is Christ, the Messiah.

Andrew brought Peter to meet Jesus. Who in your life introduced you to Jesus? How did that introduction affect your life?

Think back to how meaningful it was for you to first understand what it was like to have a personal encounter with Jesus. In John 1:42, Jesus gave Simon, Andrew's brother, a new name. How has Jesus affected your life?

Jesus clearly knew Simon Peter before Andrew brought him there. If you aren't sure about your relationship with Jesus, how does being known by him make you feel?

My prayer to God today is:

_____

_____

_____

_____

_____

_____

MICRO STUDY 3

Read John 1:43–51.

Write out John 1:46 here:

_____

_____

_____

_____

Remember the woman at the well? Imagine if she had turned on the suspicion and assumed Jesus was adding something nefarious to the living water he offered. When we have presupposed ideas about Jesus, it can leave us skeptical. Here, Nathanael wondered how someone from a forgotten town like Nazareth could truly be the One they waited for. Philip's response was, "Come and see."

Like Simon Peter's encounter, what about Nathanael's experience caught him by surprise?

When has God surprised you by knowing your needs better than you knew them yourself?

When have you doubted or questioned who Jesus is in your life? (You surely aren't alone in this!)

What hope does Nathanael's story give you about how Jesus has hopes and plans beyond your limited thinking?

My prayer to God today is:

_____

_____

_____

_____

_____

MICRO STUDY 4

Read John 2:1–11.

Write out John 2:11 here:

_____

_____

_____

_____

How does this passage challenge your perceptions about Jesus's work in your life?

As you think about spiritual refilling, consider how Jesus provided the best wine in abundance. What does this tell you about how he will provide for your soul needs?

This miracle also had an opportunity for skepticism. Imagine being one of the servants who filled jars with water and was then instructed to draw some out and bring it to the master of ceremonies. Describe how it feels to obey Jesus's instructions without understanding the outcome.

My prayer to God today is:

_____

_____

_____

_____

_____

MICRO STUDY 5

Read Philippians 1:7–11.

Write out Philippians 1:11 here:

_____

_____

_____

_____

_____

In this letter from the apostle Paul, we see a reflection of the kind of refilling and overflow Jesus spoke of in John. Specifically, Paul addressed overflowing love. Jesus's qualities will be evident when we belong to him, just as a well-watered garden produces fruit. Describe what "righteous character" looks like.

What does it mean in practical, everyday terms for our behavior to bring glory to God?

Notice that being filled with the fruit of our salvation and our relationship to God as children comes from Christ's work in us. Why is it significant to know that you don't have to accomplish this alone?

My prayer to God today is:

_____

_____

_____

_____

_____

_____

_____

_____

Hope in Action

REVIEW THE LIST YOU MADE OF THINGS that refresh you in the First Thoughts at the beginning of this chapter. If you have more to add to the list, go ahead and put those there.

Go back and put a check by the activities you make time for often. Put a plus next to the things you want to make more time for.

Make time this week to do one of the things on your list that refreshes you. If you can sneak in more than one, try to add a small thing each day. These don't have to be big or cost a lot of money. It might include some of these examples (personalized to your tastes, of course):

- A brisk walk
- A slow stroll
- Journaling or writing
- Gardening (tending plants or visiting a garden center)
- Laughing (funny movie, time with a funny friend)
- Reading Scripture
- Spending time with loved ones
- A nap in a hammock
- Reading with a cup of tea
- Prayer or meditation
- Attending a Bible study or church
- Artistic expressions
- Walking around a big city
- People watching
- Cultural experiences
- Outdoor concerts or indoor music events
- Physical exercise

Identify any barriers that stand in the way of pursuing these activities more often than you do. Perhaps you can find a way to bundle several things together. For example, listening to Scripture while you walk. Create an action plan on the next page for overcoming the obstacles that keep you from making time for refreshment.

My Plan

WEEK TWO
RECEIVE

*From his abundance we have all received
one gracious blessing after another.*
—John 1:16

First Thoughts

REFLECT ON YOUR ABILITY TO RECEIVE HELP, advice, or kindness from others. Are there barriers that prevent you from accepting what others offer? Write about what it means to be truly open to receiving and how you can cultivate that openness.

_____

_____

_____

_____

_____

_____

_____

_____

_____

_____

_____

_____

_____

_____

_____

_____

_____

_____

_____

_____

STORY

I AM NOT A RUNNER. MY THIGHS, tummy, underarms, and other parts of my body were not manufactured to flap as much as they do when I jog. Not even if all parts were to flap in sync. And mine don't. A strong dislike for chafing also keeps me from moving at a pace that could ever be defined as running. Scooting, maybe. But running, never ever.

As part of a non-running commitment to get in shape one year, I decided to walk seven 5K races in seven months—a 5K, as in five kilometers, which is more impressive than calling it the 3.1 miles it is. Those metric people have something great going for them. The distances are longer than miles when you count kilometers, and a person's body weight in kilograms is a much lower figure than it is in pounds.

Many runners finish a 5K in under twenty minutes, a blink of time and energy for a seasoned athlete. They lounge at the finish line, having bananas and milk while the rest of us press on. I finished my first race in fifty-one pathetic minutes. Despite a calf-cramping, shin-splinting pace, I was behind several women pushing double-wide strollers or carrying toddlers. Behind several people thirty years my senior. I'd have been mortified, but I did finish, at least.

GETTING LAPPED

In some races, we walkers met the runners on their return trip to the finish line long before my stubby legs reached the halfway point for the turnaround—the equivalent of getting "lapped" had we been on a track. However, by the end of that summer, I could walk a 5K in around forty-five minutes, which means I had shaved a minute off each kilometer.

Some of those races occurred in the hottest part of the summer at the peak of late-afternoon temperatures. Along the race route, volunteers lined up on both sides of the trail, arms extended with overflowing Dixie cups of water for the participants as we passed by (I'd say the athletes, but I was far from being anything but a participant). All we had to do was reach out and grab one of the extended cups and keep moving as the refreshing water dribbled down our chins and quenched our parched tongues. Some runners poured the water over their heads and let it mingle with rivers of sweat on flushed faces.

The act of receiving water in a 5K is a tangible, visible exchange with instant impact. The runner doesn't even have to ask. It's offered by someone who knows just what they need. Often, the person holding the cup also gives a few words of encouragement: "You're doing great!"

Never did I hear, "Eew! Sweaty person. Get away from me!" My messiness didn't matter.

As he did with the woman at the well, Jesus offers us divine refreshment that brings immediate relief to our dry souls. Our mess doesn't bother him either. His living water isn't a temporary relief but a continuous source of hydration that helps us persevere through life's trials and disappointments. All we have to do is receive.

The momentary pause, barely more than a blink of an eye, becomes a turning point for a runner, enabling them to push forward with revitalized determination.

This is your momentary pause. Your turning point to receive something from Jesus and let his Word hydrate your soul. It is the opportunity for lasting transformation. Will you receive what Jesus offers?

PRAYER

GOD, I'M SO GLAD YOU DON'T SAVE your gift of grace for perfect people, and I'm humbled and awed by what you can do amid my imperfections. I'm thirsty for spiritual filling. Please help me seek satisfaction in you first and not in other things. I want to receive the life you offer and be refreshed by your Spirit. As I explore your Word, show me how to apply truth and experience transformation.

EXPLORE THE WORD

IF YOU'VE PARTICIPATED IN BIBLE STUDIES FOR a long time, it's possible you have studied the story of the woman who met Jesus at a well in Samaria. Maybe you have studied it numerous times. Whether it's your first time studying this story or your twentieth, today we are going to consider how a few moments with Jesus can change everything. Last week, we focused on the gift Jesus offered: living water. Today, we'll explore what happens when we receive that gift and the Holy Spirit steps into our everyday moments.

If needed, go ahead and review John 4:3–15 in the previous lesson or in your Bible. Then, let's look at a little background about the culture of the time.

JEWISH CULTURE AND WOMEN

The rabbis of Jesus's time wouldn't typically address women publicly. Experts say, "Women were not to be saluted or spoken to in the street, and they were not to be instructed in the law."[*] Some of this may have come from a desire to make sure there was no appearance of anything improper or any potential to lead to adultery. If we were to look back at the writings and governing attitudes of the culture of Jesus's time, we would be surprised to learn that how women were portrayed in the Gospels was vastly different from the norm. Jesus set a new standard.

One chapter before this, in John 3, Jesus conversed with a highly educated Jewish male named Nicodemus, whom we'll meet in week 5. Jesus treated this woman, who was most likely illiterate, with the same respect he gave the educated Pharisee, Nicodemus.

We live in a culture where the attitudes about women are always developing, and women seek to find their voice. This is not new; it presents itself differently in each century, but the evolution of attitudes about women's roles is age-old.

> The woman came around noon rather than the customary morning or evening when it was cooler. She also came alone. These two things "suggest the woman felt a sense of shame and was avoiding contact with other women."[**]

[**] Kruse, *John*, 129.

[*] James M. Freeman and Harold J. Chadwick, *Manners & Customs of the Bible* (North Brunswick, NJ: Bridge-Logos Publishers, 1998), 514.

In the Gospels, we see Jesus raising women to an equal status with men in the message of the gospel. Their role as disciples and followers of Christ is not secondary. This equality is further underscored in the leadership of the early Christian church, where women played a significant role, as evidenced in the letters Paul wrote to the churches.

It's also important to note that the nameless woman had a second reason that made this conversation with Jesus unusual. She was a Samaritan, which meant a Jew would avoid talking with her based on religious and political differences. Let's explore that more.

THE SETTING

I always thought Jesus chose to go the longer, less desirable route. But I realized from reading multiple commentaries that this wasn't necessarily true.

The district of Samaria was between Judea and Galilee, on the west side of the Jordan River. There were three routes Jesus could have taken between Jerusalem and Galilee; two went around Samaria, and one went through it. The normal route was the latter.[*] Some Jews chose to go the long way around, but Jesus went the usual way, stopping at Sychar on the way.

The Samaritans believed in the God of the Jews, but they also held to their old beliefs in other gods. We could do another whole lesson about the troubles with believing in God and holding on to other beliefs that don't align with the Bible, but we won't digress.

"Jacob bequeathed a piece of land near here [Sychar] to his son Joseph, and it was in this land that Joseph's bones were laid to rest when the Israelites came up out of Egypt (Gen. 33:19; Josh. 24:32)."[**]

One Bible dictionary describes them as "people who believed they were the true descendants of Israel and keepers of the Torah. During the New Testament time, their chief religious site was Mount Gerizim. The Samaritans believed that the Jerusalem temple and priesthood were illegitimate."[†]

The Gospels make the hostility between Jews and Samaritans clear in brief episodes here and there. Samaritans didn't always welcome Jewish travelers in their territory. However, the traveling disciples needed food, so they went into the town.[‡]

** Kruse, *John*, 129.

* Kruse, *John*, 129.

† Maiers, "Samaritans," *The Lexham Bible Dictionary*.

‡ Kruse, *John*, 130.

Let's pick up the conversation between Jesus and the woman right after he asked her for a drink. "The woman was surprised, for Jews refuse to have anything to do with Samaritans. She said to Jesus, 'You are a Jew, and I am a Samaritan woman. Why are you asking me for a drink?'" (John 4:9).

Have you ever been surprised by a conversation? When has someone spoken to you who had reasons not to?

How did that feel?

How do you think the woman might have felt?

How does self-worth affect decisions?

Extra study: You can learn more about the Samaritans from 2 Kings 17:24–33.

Sources disagree about the origins of the Samaritans, depending on whether the source is Jewish or Samaritan. "Many of the rabbis of the Second Temple period did not consider the Samaritans as ethnically Jewish, but of Cuthean descent. The Samaritans, however, viewed themselves as descendants of the tribes of Ephraim and Manasseh, and trace their lineage to the time of Eli."[*]

* Brian Maiers, "Samaritans," in *The Lexham Bible Dictionary*, ed. John D. Barry et al. (Bellingham, WA: Lexham Press, 2016).

I do want to make it clear here that we don't really know if the woman had been divorced or widowed—or a combination of both. And we don't know if she was living with a relative or a partner to whom she wasn't married. However, the context implies something disreputable about her situation.

We've already established the two strikes of being a woman and a Samaritan. But this woman had *another* strike against her. She had a reputation, and Jesus was about to show what he knew about her.

[16] "Go and get your husband," Jesus told her.

[17] "I don't have a husband," the woman replied. Jesus said, "You're right! You don't have a husband— [18] for you have had five husbands, and you aren't even married to the man you're living with now. You certainly spoke the truth!"

[19] "Sir," the woman said, "you must be a prophet. [20] So tell me, why is it that you Jews insist that Jerusalem is the only place of worship, while we Samaritans claim it is here at Mount Gerizim, where our ancestors worshiped?"

[21] Jesus replied, "Believe me, dear woman, the time is coming when it will no longer matter whether you worship the Father on this mountain or in Jerusalem. [22] You Samaritans know very little about the one you worship, while we Jews know all about him, for salvation comes through the Jews. [23] But the time is coming—indeed it's here now—when true worshipers will worship the Father in spirit and in truth. The Father is looking for those who will worship him that way. [24] For God is Spirit, so those who worship him must worship in spirit and in truth."

[25] The woman said, "I know the Messiah is coming—the one who is called Christ. When he comes, he will explain everything to us."

[26] Then Jesus told her, "I AM the Messiah!" (John 4:16–26)

Here, the conversation took a turn. Suddenly, Jesus wasn't talking about water but the woman. They went quickly from superficial to supernatural. He started out by asking for something *from* her, but it didn't take long to see that he was there to offer something *to* her.

In her search for someone to love her, she had been with many different "husbands" (v. 18). In this respectful discussion, Jesus showed the woman her real need wasn't the love of a man but God's love.

They started discussing doctrinal things, and the woman immediately felt comfortable asking Jesus deep questions. She knew her Samaritan theology and how it differed from the Jewish beliefs. Notice how Jesus was both authoritative and loving in his response to her.

What usually happens when you and another person go straight to discussing your differing theology?

When you read verses 25–26, what comes to mind?

How might you have felt if you had been in her shoes and learned that Jesus was the one you had been waiting for to sort out the confusion?

The Samaritan woman had been searching for spiritual truth. Perhaps it had something to do with what she had sought through many relationships. Either way, the concept of forsaking God and pursuing empty sources to attempt to find meaning goes all the way back to the Old Testament. God is, and has always been, the source of life and salvation. But since the beginning of time, his people have rejected truth and his goodness and have done their own thing. The prophet Jeremiah shared this message from the Lord with the Israelites:

> "For my people have done two evil things: They have abandoned me—the fountain of living water. And they have dug for themselves cracked cisterns that can hold no water at all!" (Jeremiah 2:13)

Describe what it feels like to attempt to find satisfaction only to have it seep out through figurative cracks.

What does it feel like to be in an emotional state where you want to hide from other people?

What has it cost you to search for meaning in all the wrong places? Perhaps that includes friends, romance, things, clothing, shopping, or food.

Jesus revealed the woman's deepest secrets without her telling him anything. Notice he did not indicate any intent to create guilt or shame. He stepped into her world and showed he knew she had pain. He acknowledged her spiritual thirst but didn't shame her spiritual poverty. He never said, "You're thirsty? Shame on you for being thirsty." His words showed that he saw her thirst and had a solution.

He also revealed something about himself that she didn't know. His offer was much more than she could have imagined. He was the Messiah, the Savior of the world that she had heard was coming (vv. 25–26). The heart walls crumbled, and she heard the good news that God looked for worshippers of all backgrounds, not only those born of Jewish heritage.

Have you ever felt left out, as if certain things were only for some people? How did that affect your spiritual health (especially if you felt left out of Christian circles)?

Think about when you have had a physical need that someone anticipated for you. They handed you a glass of water before you asked or placed a plate of food in front of you. Someone gave you a blanket or offered to watch your children while you rested. How does it feel when someone notices your need?

COMPELLED TO SHARE

When Jesus revealed who he was, suddenly everything changed. She had to tell people! In ridiculously bad timing, the disciples returned with food, were shocked to find Jesus talking with a woman, and awkwardly tried to ignore it. (See John 4:27–38.)

Their foolishness could easily have distracted them from the need right in front of them. But their interruption didn't stop the Samaritan woman. She raced to the village to tell people all about Jesus while the disciples urged Jesus to eat something.

Jesus tried to explain to his friends that he was renewed by something other than food. They were confused and hilariously literal about their understanding of Jesus's statement about spiritual food and asked if someone had brought him food while they were gone.

> Meanwhile, the disciples were urging Jesus, "Rabbi, eat something."
>
> But Jesus replied, "I have a kind of food you know nothing about."
>
> "Did someone bring him food while we were gone?" the disciples asked each other.
>
> Then Jesus explained: "My nourishment comes from doing the will of God, who sent me, and from finishing his work. You know the saying, 'Four months between planting and harvest.' But I say, wake up and look around. The fields are already ripe for harvest." (John 4:31–35)

Jesus used similar figurative speech in other places. And after his death and resurrection, his disciples remembered some of those instances (John 2:22).

Have you ever had an experience where spiritual renewal was better than any food you could ever eat? Perhaps it was a time of worship that brought you close to God or a time of quiet where you heard God's voice speak to your heart. Here, Jesus said his nourishment came from doing the will of God. The disciples didn't understand what he meant here, and his figurative speech confused them.

Jesus asked his disciples to open their eyes and look around and see the spiritual harvest that was right in front of them. These Samaritans needed to know about what the Messiah offered them.

Hope.

Imagine being one of the disciples. You suddenly lift your eyes and realize that crowds of people are coming to Jesus at this moment because the woman had run to get her friends. Look at the result of her testimony.

> Many Samaritans from the village believed in Jesus be-cause the woman had said, "He told me everything I ever did!" When they came out to see him, they begged him to stay in their village. So he stayed for two days, long enough for many more to hear his message and be-lieve. Then they said to the woman, "Now we believe, not just because of what you told us, but because we have heard him ourselves. Now we know that he is in-deed the Savior of the world." (John 4:39–42)

We can learn so much from her story. Notice how this wom-an was refreshed by her new faith. And notice how Jesus's methods were gentle and kind. He didn't argue the fine points of theology or doctrine with her—even though her beliefs were entirely mixed up. He didn't condemn her for her obvious sin but offered her the solu-tion she desperately needed.

Jesus gave the woman the unconditional love and acceptance we all long for. Did he condone her sin? No. He accepted her as a per-son, as a woman, as a Samaritan, as a broken seeker of truth.

Jesus broke culture by reaching out to this particular woman—because he had a purpose. God reaches out to people, regardless of gender, race, religion, or social class.

Her actions, inspired by her encounter with Jesus, had a pro-found impact on the woman's village. Her decision to share her experience led to the transformation of many lives, a testament to the ripple effect of faith.

Where do you struggle most with acting like Jesus with people who are different from you or who are caught up in sinful patterns?

When is it difficult to accept and love them even if you don't condone their actions?

"Wake up and look around. The fields are already ripe for harvest." How do Jesus's words challenge you?

Perhaps you're in the shoes of the woman, and you're afraid to be open about your struggles because you've been shamed in the past. Who can you share with this week to take a step toward receiving grace?

This is what happens when we receive refreshment. We believe the truth, we receive grace and salvation, and then it overflows as we tell others. God used a broken woman to change the eternal course of the lives of many others. Her story pointed others to the glory of God!

She no longer cared about getting water from the well because she was filled and satisfied by what Jesus offered. She wanted everyone she knew to receive it too.

God uses imperfect people to accomplish his purposes. Before she had a chance to get her life straightened out, she was already telling people about Jesus. The minute her shame lifted, she shared the good news!

If you've hesitated to tell others how Jesus has changed you, how does this woman's story inspire you?

What if Jesus had followed the legalistic views of the Jews and he only associated with the chosen ones? After all, God sent him to rescue the Jews initially. What if he had been proper and avoided talking to a woman?

What happens when we do hard things? God uses our obedience to bring others to new life.

What happens when imperfect people listen to the urge to share the gospel? Many people are stunned by the change, and they believe too.

The apostle Paul explained why he was thankful that God considered him worthy of serving the Lord.

I thank Christ Jesus our Lord, who has given me strength to do his work. He considered me trustworthy and appointed me to serve him, even though I used to blaspheme the name of Christ. In my insolence, I persecuted his people. But God had mercy on me because I did it in ignorance and unbelief. Oh, how generous and gracious our Lord was! He filled me with the faith and love that come from Christ Jesus.

This is a trustworthy saying, and everyone should accept it: "Christ Jesus came into the world to save sinners"— and I am the worst of them all. But God had mercy on me so that Christ Jesus could use me as a prime example of his great patience with even the worst sinners. Then others will realize that they, too, can believe in him and receive eternal life. All honor and glory to God forever and ever! He is the eternal King, the unseen one who never dies; he alone is God. Amen. (1 Timothy 1:12–17)

Paul's story sounds so much like that of the Samaritan woman. "But God had mercy on me so that . . . others will realize that they, too, can believe in him and receive eternal life" (v. 16).

The Samaritan woman was refreshed by receiving the life Jesus offered—the living water of truth. Jesus loves you, imperfections and all. And he has a plan for your life. Now, that's something to celebrate!

Prayer Journal

I'M THANKFUL FOR:

_____

_____

_____

_____

_____

_____

I'M ASKING GOD FOR:

_____

_____

_____

_____

_____

_____

WORDS OF WORSHIP TO GOD:

_____

_____

_____

_____

_____

_____

APPLY

MICRO STUDY 1

Read Galatians 3:13–29.

Write out Galatians 3:28 here:

_____

_____

_____

_____

Jesus spoke with the woman at the well, offering her the same promise a Jew might receive as a descendant of Abraham (John 4). And here, the apostle Paul reminded his Christian friends in Galatia that Gentiles (non-Jews) have the promise of new life because of Jesus, who removed the curse of the law. What do you think about also being considered part of Abraham's spiritual family?

Galatians 3:27 uses the imagery of being clothed with Christ. How is this different from knowing facts about Christ?

This clothing comes with a heritage. How does recognizing our identity in Christ, rather than our outward differences, impact how we interact with and relate to others?

My prayer to God today is:

_____

_____

_____

_____

MICRO STUDY 2

Read John 12:1–11.

Write out John 12:8 here:

_____

_____

_____

_____

Notice the contrast between Judas's greed and Mary's devotion to Jesus. Judas disguised his greed by pretending to be concerned for the poor. What does Mary's posture tell us about what Jesus asks of us?

What can you learn from her extravagant act of love and devotion?

Jesus wasn't disparaging the passage that said, "There will always be some in the land who are poor. That is why I am commanding you to share freely with the poor and with other Israelites in need" (Deuteronomy 15:11). Instead, he was talking about the importance of prioritizing him above other service. Can you think of "good" activities that might keep you from giving Jesus your extravagant devotion?

My prayer to God today is:

_____

_____

_____

_____

_____

MICRO STUDY 3

Read John 12:20–26.

Write out John 12:25 here:

_____

_____

_____

_____

The idea of dying in order to live sounds backward, but Jesus's illustration of a seed is a perfect example of how faith works. The seed dies, but a new plant comes forth from the dirt. Where have you seen new life at work since surrendering control of your life to Jesus?

What do you think verse 25 means when it speaks of caring nothing for life in this world?

How might that be misconstrued or misapplied?

What is at stake if we focus only on ourselves and our life here?

What are some practical ways you can demonstrate your commitment to Jesus daily? How do your ambitions, plans, and desires fit into his plan?

My prayer to God today is:

_____

_____

_____

_____

MICRO STUDY 4

Read 1 John 2:1–14.

Write out 1 John 2:5 here:

_____

_____

_____

_____

_____

Explain why love and obedience would be tied together.

"Do not seek revenge or bear a grudge against a fellow Israelite, but love your neighbor as yourself. I am the Lord." (Leviticus 19:18)

How do you feel when someone promises to do something but doesn't? How does it affect your relationship?

John said he wasn't giving a new commandment but reiterating an old one when he said to love one another. But then he said it was also new, citing Jesus as our living truth. Describe how the cross adds a new dimension to love.

"Owe nothing to anyone—except for your obligation to love one another. If you love your neighbor, you will fulfill the requirements of God's law." (Romans 13:8)

How has loving Jesus helped you to love others more?

My prayer to God today is:

_____

_____

_____

_____

_____

MICRO STUDY 5

Read 1 John 2:15–29.

Write out 1 John 2:24 here:

_____

_____

_____

_____

_____

In terms of your experience, describe what it means to love this world and what it offers you.

Contrast that with what it looks like to live according to the Holy Spirit in your current culture. Describe the impact you can have.

When you receive Jesus, you also receive his Spirit living within you. According to verse 27, what role does the Holy Spirit play in your life?

Describe what it means to "remain in fellowship with Christ."

My prayer to God today is:

_____

_____

_____

_____

_____

Hope in Action

PLAN A SOLO RETREAT OR PARTICIPATE IN a group retreat focused on spiritual renewal and seeking God's presence. Look for one that isn't packed with activities but allows time to learn to be comfortable with silence. Set up your retreat to be free from distractions such as phones or social media and interruptions from others. Seek quiet times for prayer, meditation, reflection, and studying the Bible.

Your retreat might be a few hours, a few days, or longer. The important thing is to start with what works for you. Ideas to make your spiritual retreat meaningful:

- Pray. Ask God to show you what you need right now to help you experience his refreshment in a new way.
- Plan to be in nature, near a river or a lake, or somewhere that reminds you of the living water Jesus offers.
- Make time for walks in nature to talk with God.
- You can use books and guides, but it's also freeing to select a few Bible passages to read over several times during your retreat, allowing time to listen to God. You'll find a reading plan at the end of this book focused on the meaning of Jesus's death and resurrection.
- Use books or devotionals sparingly and prioritize reading Scripture over other people's words.
- Make a playlist of songs that inspire you in your faith.
- Sometimes, journaling helps to keep your mind from straying too far into unrelated things.
- Prioritize sleep and rest.
- Some people incorporate fasting. Others just keep meals simple.
- Try creative expression: drawing, painting, dance, music.

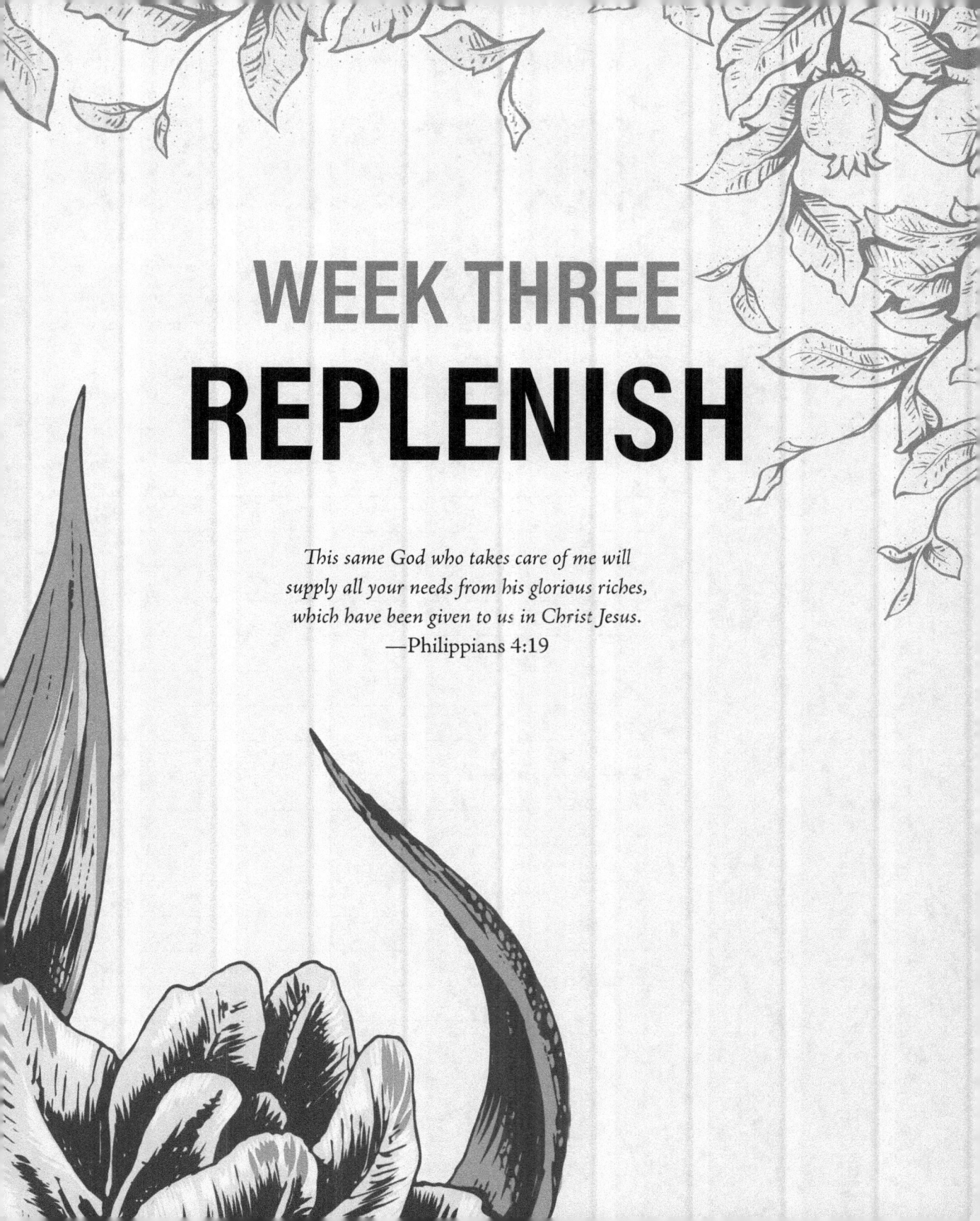

WEEK THREE
REPLENISH

*This same God who takes care of me will
supply all your needs from his glorious riches,
which have been given to us in Christ Jesus.*
—Philippians 4:19

First Thoughts

THINK ABOUT WHEN YOU HAVE FELT SPIRITUALLY, emotionally, or physically drained. How did you find renewal and replenishment during that period? Write about the steps you took or the sources of strength you relied on.

_____

_____

_____

_____

_____

_____

_____

_____

_____

_____

_____

_____

_____

_____

_____

_____

_____

_____

STORY

MY YEARS OF PARENTING TEEN BOYS WERE financially lean. We lived on my husband's ministry income and a little side income I earned from teaching piano lessons. I had to find ways to feed our family of four on a minimal grocery budget. And when the boys invited friends over to hang out, the demand for pizza, snacks, and cereal surged. We lived forty miles from a Domino's or a Jimmy John's, so even if DoorDash had been a thing, I'd have been too cheap to let anyone think of using the service.

I quickly discovered that any sort of bread was an inexpensive way to make a lot of filling food. Just a disclaimer: I am not responsible for any pancreatic deficiencies those boys—both friends and family—might have now that they are all in their thirties. And I swear I'm not responsible for one of my sons now having celiac disease and being unable to inhale even a speck of wheat flour without it inducing three days of intestinal rebellion.

Bread was cheap and filling because I could make it myself. I had a family recipe that contained no butter, eggs, or milk—the things that cost more money. It had just flour, yeast, sugar, salt, oil, and water. Surprisingly, it was soft and delicious. The kind of bread you never get tired of. Alas, let the record show that I myself can no longer eat wheat and have not savored its crusty goodness in over seven years.

Scan the code with your phone camera to get the bread recipe!

That recipe produced five huge loaves from every batch and could be used for cinnamon rolls, dinner rolls, hoagies, French bread, or pizza crust as needed. I followed generational traditions and fired up the oven at least once a week to restock the bread items. We shopped at the warehouse club to get twenty-five-pound bags of bread flour, gallon jugs of canola oil, and bulk yeast.

If you have never experienced getting off the school bus and smelling the fresh bread through the screen door before your shoes hit the front landing, I'm sorry. You missed something wonderful that included big, warm slices of bread with pats of butter melting into them. Sometimes we got a sprinkle of cinnamon sugar over the butter.

With the teens and their friends, I discovered that if I plopped a fresh loaf or two on a wooden cutting board, set out some butter and a jar of homemade jam, their snack hankering would be satisfied for a long time. They kept coming back to the dining table from the rec room to grab slices, making more than one loaf disappear each time. The jam came from the freezer, where I stored up big batches made from seasonal berries picked in our yard. With bread, jam, and butter, we continued replenishing those bottomless pits without breaking the bank.

Since ancient days, flour, oil, and water have been the staples for filling bellies and nourishing bodies. In 1 Kings 17, the prophet Elijah's needs were met by a widow who experienced miraculous provision as God kept her jars of flour and oil topped off in a famine. But unlike my efforts to feed a family on the cheap, God doesn't cheap out on meeting your spiritual needs. He becomes what satisfies your deepest needs and longings.

In a world that leaves us empty and exhausted, he wants to replenish you with everything you need to thrive. And he'll do it from an endless abundance.

> Your unfailing love, O LORD, is as vast as the heavens;
> your faithfulness reaches beyond the clouds.
> Your righteousness is like the mighty mountains,
> your justice like the ocean depths.
> You care for people and animals alike, O LORD.
> How precious is your unfailing love, O God!
> All humanity finds shelter
> in the shadow of your wings.
> You feed them from the abundance of your own house,
> letting them drink from your river of delights.
> For you are the fountain of life,
> the light by which we see. (Psalm 36:5–9)

PRAYER

GOD, I APPROACH YOU WITH AN OPEN and longing heart. I acknowledge that you are the source of all I need, and I thank you for being my provider. I ask you to fill me with your nourishment and satisfy my deepest spiritual hunger. Where I seek the things that cannot sustain me, I ask you to teach me to rely on you for all I need. Help me find refreshment in your promises and love, a spiritual renewal for my soul.

EXPLORE THE WORD

I LOVE HOW JESUS USED ANALOGIES RELATED to the basics we need to sustain life: food and water. We've studied living water, and today, we'll talk about bread. We'll begin in chapter 6 of the book of John. Some of the passage will be printed in the discussion, but if you have your Bible open, you'll be able to see the parts that I summarized too.

Jesus was becoming a popular guy. Who wouldn't want to follow someone who healed people and performed many miracles! Jesus sailed across the Sea of Galilee, climbed a hill, sat down with his disciples, and instantly a crowd gathered (John 6:1–3). As an introvert, the thought of having crowds chase me gives me anxiety. I can relate to Jesus's times of solitude more than the crowds.

Jesus asked the question that crosses my mind and also gives me angst whenever a bunch of people stop by our house: What are we going to feed them? Some of my friends have a plan for such an occasion. I seldom plan well for drop-in company.

However, Jesus already had a plan. As you read the following verses, underline each response that implies a that's-not-gonna-work attitude.

Mark 6:30–44 provides another account of this story. There, Jesus asked them to sit in groups of hundreds and fifties. His sense of organization really speaks to my appreciation for administrative gifts.

⁵ Jesus soon saw a huge crowd of people coming to look for him. Turning to Philip, he asked, "Where can we buy bread to feed all these people?" ⁶ He was testing Philip, for he already knew what he was going to do.

⁷ Philip replied, "Even if we worked for months, we wouldn't have enough money to feed them!"

⁸ Then Andrew, Simon Peter's brother, spoke up. ⁹ "There's a young boy here with five barley loaves and two fish. But what good is that with this huge crowd?"

¹⁰ "Tell everyone to sit down," Jesus said. So they all sat down on the grassy slopes. (The men alone numbered about 5,000.) ¹¹ Then Jesus took the loaves, gave thanks to God, and distributed them to the people. Afterward he did the same with the fish. And they all ate as much as they wanted. ¹² After everyone was full, Jesus told his disciples, "Now gather the leftovers, so that nothing is wasted." ¹³ So they picked up the pieces and filled twelve baskets with scraps left by the people who had eaten from the five barley loaves. (John 6:5–13)

What do you learn about Jesus's nature here when you see that he already had a plan but was testing Philip (v. 6)?

What does Philip's response show you about his beliefs about Jesus?

Have you ever demonstrated a similar belief by responding to something God prompted you to do? Describe it.

Based on what you know about God throughout the whole Bible, what would you say in response to Andrew's question, which included, "What good is that?" (v. 9).

What does everyone eating as much as they wanted (v. 11) teach you about how God provides?

The word *replenish* means to fully supply, make full again, or build up again. It also means to fill with inspiration and power.* There were even leftovers after everyone was "fully supplied" with food—and not with nibbles or a snack but with as much as they wanted. Of course, Andrew's response was logical. Thinking a tiny lunch could satisfy all those people was ludicrous.

Notice how Jesus used that absurd contrast to make a point. It wasn't as if they had a banquet for 4500 and wondered if they could

---

* *Merriam-Webster's Collegiate Dictionary*, s.v. "replenish," accessed August 18, 2023, https://unabridged. merriam-webster.com/collegiate/replenish.

stretch it to 5000—which was even more, considering that was only the number of men. No, Jesus took food for *one*. One person's very inadequate meal plus the disciples' very inadequate faith. And he replenished everyone's stomachs from that.

This miracle did nothing to suppress the crowd's enthusiasm. They had followed Jesus there. "When the people saw him do this miraculous sign, they exclaimed, 'Surely, he is the Prophet we have been expecting!' When Jesus saw that they were ready to force him to be their king, he slipped away into the hills by himself" (John 6:14–15).

RETREAT

Jesus slipped away by himself. That evening, his disciples waited by the boat. It was time to head back home, but he was nowhere to be found. Now, it was getting dark, and they made the decision to leave without him.

> But as darkness fell and Jesus still hadn't come back, they got into the boat and headed across the lake toward Capernaum. Soon a gale swept down upon them, and the sea grew very rough. They had rowed three or four miles when suddenly they saw Jesus walking on the water toward the boat. They were terrified, but he called out to them, "Don't be afraid. I am here!" Then they were eager to let him in the boat, and immediately they arrived at their destination! (John 6:17–21)

I live a two-hour drive south of Lake Superior. My husband and I have made an annual tradition of taking a vacation at the beginning of the period called the gales of November. Historically, many vessels have shipwrecked on the rocks along the shoreline during the gales season. We once experienced waterfront waves swelling enough to blast the second-story condominium windows with lake stones.

I sometimes stare at the waves pounding a few yards from the deck of our rented condo, pondering how awful it would be to be in a boat. Frankly, the thoughts bring a sense of panic despite the safety inside by the fire. So, I cannot imagine how the disciples felt. And they were *rowing*. This wasn't the kind of vessel that powers through wicked waves.

Describe what being in a boat in the dark on rough seas might be like.

"The Sea of Galilee lies about six hundred feet below sea level. Cool air from the south-eastern tablelands can rush in to displace the warm moist air over the lake, churning up the water in a violent squall."[*]

Now, picture Jesus walking on the water toward you. This passage says they were terrified, but not of the waves. If we aren't sure from reading it here, we can look in Mark 6:49 to see that they thought Jesus was a ghost when they saw him.

Notice what he said to calm their fears: "I am here." Some translations say, "It is I." The NLT footnote says the Greek equivalent is "The I AM is here."

This is similar to God's use of "I AM" when the Lord appeared to Moses when he was also afraid (Exodus 3:14).[†]

Why were Jesus's words comforting to them?

---

[*] D. A. Carson, *The Gospel according to John*, The Pillar New Testament Commentary (Leicester, England; Grand Rapids, MI: Inter-Varsity Press; W.B. Eerdmans, 1991), 275.

[†] *Holy Bible: New Living Translation* (Carol Stream, IL: Tyndale House Publishers, 2015), Jn 6:20.

What did the whole situation show about Jesus's majesty?

The Gospel of Mark says the wind stopped when Jesus got into the boat. The disciples were amazed, but even after the miracle with the bread and fish, they still didn't "understand the significance of the miracle of the loaves" (Mark 6:52). Neither did the crowds of people. They hopped into boats and went back across the lake the next day, searching for Jesus.

Imagine their confusion upon finding him in Capernaum. They hadn't seen him leave with the disciples, yet here he was.

Why do you think they were chasing him?

If you've ever been to an event with free food, you know what likely happened here. Jesus multiplied one tiny lunch, and suddenly he became the most popular caterer in town. There was a big difference between seeking him to replenish their physical bodies—for superficial reasons—and seeking him for deeper, spiritual reasons. The people were essentially saying, "Hey, where's the food truck?"

Imagine if Jesus had said, "Hold up! Are you here for the miracle or for the munchies?"

> Jesus replied, "I tell you the truth, you want to be with me because I fed you, not because you understood the miraculous signs. But don't be so concerned about perishable things like food. Spend your energy seeking the eternal life that the Son of Man can give you. For God the Father has given me the seal of his approval."
>
> They replied, "We want to perform God's works, too. What should we do?"
>
> Jesus told them, "This is the only work God wants from you: Believe in the one he has sent."
>
> They answered, "Show us a miraculous sign if you want us to believe in you. What can you do? After all, our ancestors ate manna while they journeyed through the

wilderness! The Scriptures say, 'Moses gave them bread from heaven to eat.'"

Jesus said, "I tell you the truth, Moses didn't give you bread from heaven. My Father did. And now he offers you the true bread from heaven. The true bread of God is the one who comes down from heaven and gives life to the world."

"Sir," they said, "give us that bread every day." (John 6:26–34)

Does the irony of the request to show them a miraculous sign hit you too? Isn't that exactly what he *had* done the day before this? He used his supernatural provision of perishable food to point to eternal life that never perishes. Seek the eternal, not the edible, he basically said. But they got stuck there on the consumables. He had healed sick bodies and turned water into wine. But that hadn't convinced them either.

What does the crowd's response tell you about their understanding of "true bread" and how to get it?

"When the crowd saw Jesus provide food for them miraculously in the wilderness, they identified him as the Prophet like Moses [John 6:14], but it seems they were expecting something more spectacular than what they had already witnessed. Jewish people in the first century spoke of Moses as the one who gave the manna from heaven (in cooperation with God), and were looking for a second Moses/Redeemer who would do the same."[*]

---

[*] Kruse, *John*, 168–169.

What does their response reveal about people's ideas of what God wants from them?

This conversation about eating his flesh and drinking his blood in John 6:51–58 might explain why some people believe that with Lord's Supper/Eucharist the elements literally become Jesus's body and blood. One commentator said, "It is understandable how people might make this connection after the institution of the Lord's Supper, but Jesus' words here must be interpreted in their own context, which clearly indicates that eating his flesh and drinking his blood is a striking metaphor for believing in him. Those who believe in him benefit from his death on their behalf."[*]

---

[*] Kruse, *John*, 176.

Jesus explained how he had come to do God's will (John 6:37–40). And when he said he had been sent from heaven, they hit a speed bump.

> Then the people began to murmur in disagreement because he had said, "I am the bread that came down from heaven." They said, "Isn't this Jesus, the son of Joseph? We know his father and mother. How can he say, 'I came down from heaven'?" (John 6:41–42)

The objection wasn't so much about calling himself bread but about claiming to be from heaven when he was Joseph's son. And then things got even more confusing.

> "I tell you the truth, anyone who believes has eternal life. Yes, I am the bread of life! Your ancestors ate manna in the wilderness, but they all died. Anyone who eats the bread from heaven, however, will never die. I am the living bread that came down from heaven.
>
> Anyone who eats this bread will live forever; and this bread, which I will offer so the world may live, is my flesh." Then the people began arguing with each other about what he meant. "How can this man give us his flesh to eat?" they asked. (John 6:47–52)

I can see why this was a little weird for the people. After that, he started talking about eating his flesh and drinking his blood. He continued with the shock factor, saying, "I am the true bread that came down from heaven. Anyone who eats this bread will not die as your ancestors did (even though they ate the manna) but will live forever" (v. 58).

He sure loved a good metaphor, didn't he? Look at the following verses.

> For it is my Father's will that all who see his Son and believe in him should have eternal life. I will raise them up at the last day. (John 6:40)

So Jesus said again, "I tell you the truth, unless you eat the flesh of the Son of Man and drink his blood, you cannot have eternal life within you." (John 6:53)

What do you find interesting or surprising about Jesus's words?

> "Eating his flesh and drinking his blood symbolize the response of human beings for Jesus' giving himself on the cross in terms of coming to him to satisfy their hunger and believing in him to quench their thirst."[*]

*Jey J. Kanagaraj, *John*, ed. Michael F. Bird and Craig Keener, vol. 4, New Covenant Commentary Series (Eugene, OR: Cascade Books, 2013), 73–74.

It might be easy to criticize people who couldn't see what was right before their eyes. But can you think of a situation where you were that way toward God too? Where you missed his obvious presence?

What pursuit or fascination with only earthly value do you sense God asking you to deprioritize in favor of deepening your eternal relationship with him?

Jesus promised there would be no spiritual starvation or dehydration for anyone who comes to him and believes in him (John 6:35). He wants to meet your deepest spiritual need with the strength, peace, and confidence that can only come from his unlimited supply.

Prayer Journal

I'M THANKFUL FOR:

_____
_____
_____
_____
_____
_____

I'M ASKING GOD FOR:

_____
_____
_____
_____
_____
_____

WORDS OF WORSHIP TO GOD:

_____
_____
_____
_____
_____
_____

APPLY

MICRO STUDY 1

Read Psalm 36.

Write out Psalm 36:8–9 here:

_____

_____

_____

_____

_____

_____

_____

When you see how God provides for and nurtures humans, animals, and the earth, what does it teach you about his nature?

> For the word of the Lord holds true, and we can trust everything he does. He loves whatever is just and good; the unfailing love of the Lord fills the earth. (Psalm 33:4–5)

Where have you seen God replenish you spiritually when you needed his abundance in your insufficiency?

Verse 8 speaks of God's river of delights, which has the same root letters as Eden.* How does this imagery challenge the typical view on what delights us in life?

In what areas of your life do you struggle to trust God's unfailing love and provision and instead seek satisfaction elsewhere?

My prayer to God today is:

_____

_____

_____

_____

_____

_____

MICRO STUDY 2

Read John 10:1–16.

---

* *NIV Cultural Backgrounds Study Bible* (Grand Rapids: Zondervan, 2016), accessed on BibleGateway.com.

Write John 10:10–11 here:

_____

_____

_____

_____

_____

Jesus gave two illustrations of shepherding to help the disciples understand his role. He was "the shepherd who makes himself the 'door' to the enclosure to protect the sheep."* In addition to offering protection from predators, he is the door that allows the sheep to come and go, passing through him into safety and out to pasture.

How have you experienced Jesus as both the door and shepherd in your life?

In verse 10, the New Living Translation refers to a rich and satisfying life. How does this differ from how the world defines rich and satisfying?

What are some of the "thieves" that try to steal or destroy the life Jesus has given you?

---

* Kruse, *John*, 232.

How well would you say you know your Shepherd's voice? Identify several ways you can differentiate his voice from others who would lead you astray.

My prayer to God today is:

_____

_____

_____

_____

_____

MICRO STUDY 3

Read Isaiah 40:1–11.

Write out Isaiah 40:11 here:

_____

_____

_____

_____

_____

Throughout Scripture, God uses the image of a shepherd feeding a flock. In some places, David received that title. In others, it was God the Father searching for and rescuing his people (Ezekiel 34:11–16). Or, as in Isaiah, we see an image of the Lord gathering his flock close to his heart.

Describe your thoughts about the gentle leading you see in verse 11.

How does this verse reflect Psalm 23, which speaks of a shepherd providing for every need?

How can the message of hope and restoration in these verses encourage you to trust God's promises during times of difficulty or waiting?

My prayer to God today is:

_____

_____

_____

_____

_____

_____

And he will stand to lead his flock with the LORD's strength, in the majesty of the name of the LORD his God. Then his people will live there undisturbed, for he will be highly honored around the world. (Micah 5:4)

MICRO STUDY 4

Read 2 Corinthians 9.

Write out 2 Corinthians 9:10 here:

_____

_____

_____

_____

_____

_____

When you consider God's provision for every need, how does this affect your attitude toward material possessions and wealth?

When has God's generosity exceeded your expectations?

How did that strengthen your faith and trust in God?

Verse 10 speaks of seed eventually becoming the grain that can be turned into bread. This takes time. What are your thoughts on this long process versus our tendency to want something right now?

God uses others to provide for the needs of fellow humans. What is the result of generosity in verses 12–13?

My prayer to God today is:

_____

_____

_____

_____

_____

MICRO STUDY 5

Read 1 Kings 17:8–16.

Write out 1 Kings 17:16 here:

_____

_____

_____

Jesus mentioned this story during his ministry too! He said, "Certainly there were many needy widows in Israel in Elijah's time, when the heavens were closed for three and a half years, and a severe famine devastated the land. Yet Elijah was not sent to any of them. He was sent instead to a foreigner—a widow of Zarephath in the land of Sidon" (Luke 4:25–26).

Have you ever been in a situation where you had to trust God to provide for you? How did it work out?

Have you ever encountered a situation where God's supernatural provision was so evident that it defied all logical explanations?

Faith and generosity go hand in hand in this example. And God provided for the woman's needs, even though she wasn't sure what would happen. She wasn't even a believer in Elijah's God yet! Sometimes God blesses faithfulness, and it eventually becomes faith. When have you trusted God with a little or a big step and it grew your faith in leaps and bounds?

My prayer to God today is:

_____

_____

_____

_____

_____

Hope in Action

WHAT UNSATISFYING HABITS KEEP YOU FROM NURTURING your soul with the goodness God offers? Consider a possible habit change. Identify the area that needs action, then write out what you will replace it with. Put a star by one of the following, or write in your own:

- A media makeover (TV or entertainment consumption)
- Digital detox (social media habits or online activities)
- Thought transformation (negativity, bitterness, anger, etc.)
- Cluttered space (hoarding possessions)
- Achievement or success-driven without purpose
- Body obsession
- Money obsession
- Social status and popularity
- Influence and power-driven
- Toxic romance and relationships
- Substance abuse
- Pleasure-seeking habits
- Overworking or busyness
- Filling schedule to avoid deeper reflections
- Going through religious rituals without meaning
- Obsessing about politics or the news
- Other: _____

Write your plan on the next page.

My plan of action:

WEEK FOUR
RECLAIM

*Concerning the Gentiles, God says in the prophecy
of Hosea, "Those who were not my people, I will
now call my people. And I will love those whom
I did not love before." And, "Then, at the place
where they were told, 'You are not my people,' there
they will be called 'children of the living God.'"*
—Romans 9:25–26

First Thoughts

IN THE LINES BELOW, LIST THE FALSEHOODS and negative statements about yourself that sometimes run through your head. Include those that come from cultural pressures and those that the devil wants you to believe. Also, include things you *think* others might believe about you—even if logic says they don't.

_____

_____

_____

_____

_____

_____

_____

_____

Our upbringing often burdens us with false labels. These labels can stem from a past figure who failed to speak love and truth or from the echoes of our own experiences. They might even be misperceptions of others' thoughts about us. You might feel worthless, ashamed, rejected, hopeless, misunderstood, or unwanted, but these are not the truths that Jesus sees in you.

Now list the words you know to be true because of how God created you and views you. Include even the ones you have a difficult time believing.

_____

_____

_____

_____

_____

_____

_____

_____

_____

_____

_____

_____

Jesus says you are loved, free, blessed, significant, and so much more. These are not just words but scriptural truths about who we are when we belong to Jesus Christ.

STORY

BOOKLOVER. WORD NERD. ART FREAK. MASTER GARDENER. Hopeless romantic. Creative genius. Comedian. Techie. Those are lighthearted and positive labels we might be willing to make into a T-shirt. They are the fun and vibrant ones that showcase our personalities. And we aren't too upset when they stick.

Perhaps you've noticed how difficult it is to remove price stickers from Goodwill merchandise. I'm not kidding! There are online tutorials for how to remove those pink, blue, and green labels without destroying the vintage treasure you just bought. I've learned that other labels stick better than the Goodwill price tags. The ones that stay put no matter how much emotional Goo Gone we try.

ANGRY LIKE MY MOM

TRASHED BY LIFE

LOSER

Does your dialogue with others reflect defeatist tones similar to these? No one puts these on a T-shirt, but some of you are probably wearing these captions right now.

POOR SELF-IMAGE. IT'S JUST WHO I AM.

MESSED UP. AGAIN.

ETERNAL PESSIMIST

CAN'T HELP WHO I AM

FAILURE WITH A CAPITAL F

I'LL NEVER CHANGE. WHY TRY?

Did you know self-loathing statements make it easier to give in to temptation? If you believe you're a loser, how hard will you try to win? If you believe you're a hopeless cause, then why bother with trying to do the right thing?

DUSTING OFF THE PAST

Imagine your life as an attic packed with a lot of boxes, all labeled with what's inside. Some contain joys and triumphs. Others contain mistakes and failures. Past hurts. It's like your own time capsule featuring memories that make you smile, weep, or reflect. If you've ever sorted through attic boxes, you know there will be many what-in-the-world moments. Or, as my husband would say, "What the wiggity wack is this?"

I love finding ways to reclaim old stuff and make it into something different. If I discover a lonesome vintage roller skate at a yard sale, you can be sure I'll bring it home to tip it on end and affix a jar from my recycling bin. In no time, it will hold cut flowers from my yard. A rusty, bent bicycle rim will definitely become a wreath after I wire a few artificial greens around the edge.

This week, we will blow the dust off some of the boxes, take a peek at the labels, and see what's there. Our past is not made up of just random bits of clutter that ought to be tossed out like unwanted junk. As the master Artist, God reclaims it, helps us identify each hurt, and turns broken shards into a mosaic of redemption.

Think about it. Jesus didn't come to erase your history but to redeem it, as in *paid* a high price for it to exchange the broken stuff for something better.

The first book in the REMADE series, *Renewed*, focused on the dramatic transformation Jesus made in the apostle Paul. Imagine if Paul had used the excuse, "I was once a Pharisee. I'll always be legalistic and judge people; it's just who I am. It's in my DNA."

It sounds so silly when we say it that way. And yet, it's what we do when we rationalize our own boxes of junk and keep the labels.

A NEW PERSON

God has reclaimed my heart in surprising ways. I don't feel like the same person. Most people who know me probably don't see it as dramatic because a lot of the work took place in the attic—in the dark places in my heart and mind that no one gets to see.

When we repainted the outside of our house one summer, I spent a lot of evenings out front with a paintbrush, alongside my husband, covering one little patch at a time. A lot of traffic passes our house. People would roll down their windows and offer compliments. They honked and waved and gave thumbs up. They could see the progress over the years as the century-old place got a new roof, all new windows—and then paint.

But they have no idea what goes on inside. No one honks when I clear a bunch of clutter from the basement. Only the garbage man knows. No one shouts from a car window about the marvelous job we did with the backsplash or bathtub.

Many of the people who know me have very little idea about the renovation God has done in my own attitudes. They don't know what has been reclaimed and repurposed from the attic of my mind. Only those I have invited inside know what has transpired there.

As God reclaims aspects of your life, it might not be as splashy as some renovations. And don't be surprised if you stumble upon some stuff that makes you cringe. But those moments were made for grace. Grab a flashlight. There's a space in you waiting to be reclaimed, renovated, and transformed into a masterpiece.

PRAYER

THANK YOU, GOD, FOR SEEING THE VALUE in broken people. I'm so grateful for our hope and freedom in Jesus and for how you lift us up and refresh our weary souls. Help me sort through old and new labels and show me how you reclaim what I have believed to be hopeless. Discard any thoughts that I am unloved or unwanted and replace them with your beautiful truth. Empower me to release the labels that have kept me from experiencing the life you offer. Amen.

EXPLORE THE WORD

IN WEEK 1, WE LOOKED AT A passage where Jesus compared himself with living water (John 7:37–39). Let's review a little backstory here before diving into John chapter 8. It was already a controversial point of Jesus's ministry. John 7 gives us a picture of how he had been traveling around Galilee and staying out of Judea because Jewish leaders were already plotting his death. We also looked at how he snuck into the background of a festival to hear what people had been saying about him. They had all sorts of labels for who they thought Jesus was!

Some said he was a "good man." Others said, "He's nothing but a fraud who deceives the people." Many were afraid to speak the truth because of what the Jewish leaders might do to them (John 7:12–13). Jesus's response—when he finally got up to teach—was to acknowledge who he was and where he came from, but that wasn't where he stopped. "I'm not here on my own. The one who sent me is true, and you don't know him" (v. 28).

That's the core of the matter. They had questioned how he could teach without formal training from a recognized Jewish teacher (v. 15), and yet his "rabbi" had been God the Father (v. 16). Jesus's teaching didn't sit well with the Pharisees when they heard about what was happening at the temple. Therefore, "they and the leading priests sent Temple guards to arrest Jesus" (v. 32).

Jesus confused those Jewish leaders with his statements and—dare I say—intrigued them because they returned to the Pharisees without Jesus.

> When the Temple guards returned without having arrested Jesus, the leading priests and Pharisees demanded, "Why didn't you bring him in?"
>
> "We have never heard anyone speak like this!" the guards responded.
>
> "Have you been led astray, too?" the Pharisees mocked. "Is there a single one of us rulers or Pharisees who believes in him? This foolish crowd follows him, but they are ignorant of the law. God's curse is on them!" (John 7:45–49)

GUILTY BY ASSOCIATION

The meeting of Jewish leaders broke up, and everyone went home. And now, we come to this week's focal passage. We'll see how the Pharisees attempted to entrap Jesus here in John 8:1–11:

> Jesus returned to the Mount of Olives, but early the next morning he was back again at the Temple. A crowd soon gathered, and he sat down and taught them. As he was speaking, the teachers of religious law and the Pharisees brought a woman who had been caught in the act of adultery. They put her in front of the crowd.
>
> "Teacher," they said to Jesus, "this woman was caught in the act of adultery. The law of Moses says to stone her. What do you say?"
>
> They were trying to trap him into saying something they could use against him, but Jesus stooped down and wrote in the dust with his finger. They kept demanding an answer, so he stood up again and said, "All right, but let the one who has never sinned throw the first stone!" Then he stooped down again and wrote in the dust.

When the accusers heard this, they slipped away one by one, beginning with the oldest, until only Jesus was left in the middle of the crowd with the woman. Then Jesus stood up again and said to the woman, "Where are your accusers? Didn't even one of them condemn you?"

"No, Lord," she said.

And Jesus said, "Neither do I. Go and sin no more."

Adultery, as presented here, has been defined in different ways by various commentators. Some say she was a married woman. Others say she was probably betrothed rather than married. She may have even been a mistress.

As her heart pounded, waiting for the verdict, what thoughts do you think this woman had of Jesus? Based on her experience with those who represented religion, what do you think she might have expected from Jesus?

Describe what it would feel like to be this woman standing next to Jesus in shame. How does it feel to be released from that guilt and sent to go free?

Let's look at the story a little bit more. Jesus was there early in the morning teaching again, and the teachers of religious law and the Pharisees dragged a woman in who had been "caught in the act of adultery." We don't know the exact circumstances, but we could put some pieces together and speculate. Based on the early hour, this woman had probably been caught in the home and in the bed of a man who wasn't her husband, or maybe she was caught sneaking out of his home after spending the night with him.

Either way, they were not a married couple. We don't have enough information to know all the details. And that's okay because we can see just enough pieces of her story to see reflections of our own stories in her.

By law, a man and a woman who were guilty of adultery could be stoned if there were two witnesses of the sin and there was clear evidence (see Leviticus 20:10). Adultery is mentioned in the Ten Commandments in Exodus 20:14, and Jesus discussed it more in the sermon recorded in Matthew 5:27–30. There is no argument here about whether this woman was right or wrong; her accusers had evidence to prove her sin.

CAUGHT IN A TRAP

By bringing her to Jesus, the religious leaders wanted to test his knowledge of the law and his commitment to carrying out the punishment demanded by the law. Note, though, it doesn't mention that they brought the man, even though he was also guilty.

Consider their motive in dragging her into the temple. They wanted to shame her while trapping Jesus. What does this say about the Pharisees?

Contrast this with Jesus's compassion. Describe what his compassion would feel like for your struggle.

Why is this a trap? On one hand, if Jesus had answered, "Stone her," they might have charged him with being inconsistent. One commentator said, "Had He not established a reputation as one who circulated among sinners to forgive them? Might He also have crossed swords with Roman authorities, since they alone reserved the right to enact capital punishment? If on the other hand Jesus simply dismissed the Mosaic Law, He would have laid himself open to the charge of being a lawbreaker, one who disregarded the will of God as revealed to Moses."[*]

*Joseph Dongell, *John: A Bible Commentary in the Wesleyan Tradition* (Indianapolis, IN: Wesleyan Publishing House, 1997), 114.

If you have ever felt God was disappointed with you, can you identify the root of that thinking?

(Continued)

N. T. Wright gives a similar version: "They suspected that he would want to tell the woman that her sins had been forgiven; but that would mean that he would be teaching people to ignore something in the law of Moses."[*]

These Pharisees could discredit Jesus as a teacher if they could get him to say or do something contrary to the law. Remember what we already know about Pharisees and their love for the law. This would make their day if they could condemn a woman and entrap Jesus all at once.

They put the woman in front of the crowd, holding stones in their hands, ready to throw them.

"Teacher," they said to Jesus, "this woman was caught in the act of adultery. The law of Moses says to stone her. What do you say?" (vs. 4).

Imagine their tone of sarcasm as they called Jesus *teacher* and then threw the law of Moses in his face. Teacher would ordinarily be a respectful way to address him, but in this case, it was part of their scheme to entrap Jesus. They laid the trap by first acknowledging him as an authority and then presenting him with a problem they believed would put him in a dilemma.

How did Jesus's response challenge the crowd's intentions to stone the woman? What does it reveal about his forgiveness?

[*] N. T. (Tom) Wright, *John for Everyone, Part 1: Chapters 1–10* (London: Society for Promoting Christian Knowledge, 2004), 112.

How is this example significant for you when you think of times when you've fallen short of God's standard in your own life?

What did Jesus write in the dirt? N. T. Wright explained the cultural background: "In the ancient world, teachers often used to write or draw in the dust; that's how some of the great geometry teachers would explain things, in the days before chalkboards and overhead projectors."[*] Many commentators speculate on what he wrote, but all land on the idea that it doesn't matter. The main point is his actions exposed the hypocrisy of the religious leaders.

———————————

* N. T. Wright, *John for Everyone, Part 1*, 113.

It is important to acknowledge that scribes and Pharisees saw following the law as a way of expressing their devotion to God. Their motive was way off here, but I do want to point out that, once again, it was initial goodness gone awry that had them in this messed-up thinking.

In their minds, Jesus was absolutely trapped. He was about to break either civil law (ordering the death penalty for the woman without Roman authorization) or God's law (violating Deuteronomy 22:22), and either way, they were going to be rid of him. It appears they were so joyful because they believed this was foolproof.

COMPASSION WINS

Jesus didn't fall for their trap. The most important thing to note was that Jesus looked past the law, past the motive of these religious leaders, and looked straight to the woman's need. We don't know what he wrote in the dirt, but it doesn't matter.

Put yourself in this woman's place. Maybe you have felt it before. You've been dragged out in front of people and exposed for the purpose of pointing out your sins. You're ashamed, and everyone is looking at you. There is a real possibility that punishment—in her case, death, and in yours some other consequence—is about to come, and your heart pounds with fear. You're wearing a label—sinner. It's about as giant as a label can be, and it's ugly.

Imagine being so broken and standing in God's holy place—in his very temple. Disheveled, terrified, disgraced. What words describe how this feels?

Some people use John 8:7 to say we should never make moral judgments about others' behavior. That doesn't align with the rest of Scripture. "Let the one who has never sinned throw the first stone" has more to do with moral superiority. Jesus pointed out that if they wanted to be serious enough about following the law of Moses, they would have to begin with themselves.

And then Jesus forced every person in the crowd and each accuser to examine themselves. He pushed the penalty aside and pointed to their own consciences. He didn't claim she wasn't guilty; he simply asked each of her accusers to throw a stone only if they were without sin themselves.

When the accusers heard this, they slipped away one by one, beginning with the oldest, until only Jesus was left in the middle of the crowd with the woman (v. 9).

One by one, they left.

Imagine yourself in the woman's shoes. Now it's you and Jesus. No one else. Remove the voices of the people who labeled you in the past. Remove the shame that is inside your head. Remove the trap of legalism. As each "walks away," you're finally left with you and Jesus. What do you hear him say to you in that moment?

Is he throwing a stone? No. He's telling you to go and sin no more.

Deuteronomy 17:7 says, "The witnesses must throw the first stones, and then all the people may join in. In this way, you will purge the evil from among you." This would explain Jesus's comment about throwing the first stone.

How did Jesus's words and actions show that he wasn't saying he approved of her sin?

How might the woman's encounter with Jesus change her future perspective and actions?

Jesus held the woman responsible for her choices and actions. She could change the course of her life. Describe how Jesus's forgiveness has helped you change the course of your life.

ONE STONE AWAY FROM A PHARISEE

And what about the religious men who had brought her to Jesus? Maybe you've stood in their shoes before. It's easy to condemn others for their sins while justifying our own as "not that bad." We can get caught up in rules and laws and not notice the stones we hold in our hands.

Jesus gave us such a beautiful example of grace and mercy here. We don't have to excuse sin, but we don't need to condemn the sinner either. Grace means there was nothing she did to deserve the freedom Jesus gave her, but he gave it anyway. Mercy was that he didn't give her the punishment she deserved for her actions according to the law.

Do you think she danced as she left the temple? Did she walk taller and carry herself with dignity? Did she go and show others the same mercy and grace she had received?

We don't know. But consider the new labels this woman wore after meeting Jesus.

We know she was forgiven. List some other aspects of her identity that shine because of this encounter with Jesus.

Think about the labels we can wear because Jesus offers grace even when we don't deserve it. Because of Jesus, we can wear: Forgiven. Free. Clean. Loved. List some other ones that are part of your identity because of Jesus.

If it feels as if you have people all around you who would fire a stone at you at any time, look for Jesus in the crowd. He isn't holding a stone.

If you're the one standing in the crowd with a stone in your hand, ready to condemn someone else for their wrongs, set it down and examine your own heart.

The teachers of the law and the Pharisees who held those stones could have received the same grace and mercy if they also believed in Jesus. They could also have a new name! Instead of *accuser*, they could be forgiven and free to wear the name of *disciple*.

RENAMED AND RECLAIMED

Look at the verses from John 8 again.

> Then Jesus stood up again and said to the woman, "Where are your accusers? Didn't even one of them condemn you?"

"No, Lord," she said.

And Jesus said, "Neither do I. Go and sin no more." (vv. 10–11)

Notice he gave her a charge. He didn't end with forgiveness. Instead, he reclaimed a new life for her.

When I rescue a vintage roller skate or bicycle wheel for one of the projects mentioned earlier, I don't just save it from the trash heap. I reclaim it for a new purpose. Before fixing it up, I see the potential there. Jesus's command to "Go" was to leave her life of sin.

We don't know her name, but we know her previous label: "a woman caught in sin." *Sinner* is a label given to people stuck in sin habits. But we don't need to remain stuck. Is it realistic to believe we will never sin after we decide to follow Christ? No. But *sinner* doesn't need to be our name.

Christians have been called saints throughout history. The word *saint* originates from the Greek word *agios*, which is sometimes translated as saint but also as the people of God, believers, and the Lord's holy people.* This title isn't reserved for special people, as we might assume from past tradition, but is given to all believers.

When you heard the word *saint*, what was your first thought? How have you heard that word used in the past, compared to how it was described in this lesson?

---

*John R. Kohlenberger III, N*IV Exhaustive Concordance Dictionary* (Grand Rapids: Zondervan, 2015), accessed via BibleGateway.com.

Jesus told the woman in the story to go and sin no more. Why would Jesus have said this if it were impossible to stop sinning? In essence, he gave the woman a new name and a new opportunity. He changed her identity from sinner to set apart. It's as if he told her to go and be holy. It's similar to what Jesus told a crowd of people, "If any of you wants to be my follower, you must give up your own way, take up your cross daily, and follow me" (Luke 9:23).

Jesus's charge to us might be something like this. Go, live a life of victory, choosing daily to pursue holiness over the sinful desires that creep up in your thoughts. Embrace your new identity and live as a child of God who sometimes sins but pursues holiness at all costs.

The woman in the story no longer wore a label for her adultery. Instead, she could wear the labels of *holy* and *set apart*—someone who knows the peace of forgiveness and mercy. This forgiveness and mercy are for you too.

What name have you been calling yourself? Is this a label that reflects the truth of who you are in Jesus?

We can learn to live in the truth of who we really are. When tempted to get angry, we can tell ourselves, "Anger belongs to the old me." When we are tempted to worry, we can remind ourselves that worry belongs to our old self. When we are tempted by self-destructive habits, we can remember that our old self was crucified with Christ. We are renamed and reclaimed as God's children.

Prayer Journal

I'M THANKFUL FOR:

_____

_____

_____

_____

_____

_____

I'M ASKING GOD FOR:

_____

_____

_____

_____

_____

_____

WORDS OF WORSHIP TO GOD:

_____

_____

_____

_____

_____

_____

APPLY

MICRO STUDY 1

Read John 8:31–47.

Write out John 8:32 here:

_____

_____

Jesus reclaimed you as a member of his family! Describe the difference between a slave and a child.

Not everyone liked the truth Jesus presented. How did you feel if you've had someone point out truth and you weren't ready to receive it?

How does it shake your identity to admit you're wrong about something?

Describe the freedom you have experienced due to following God's truth.

My prayer to God today is:

_____

_____

_____

_____

MICRO STUDY 2

Read John 11:30–44.

Write out John 11:40 here:

_____

_____

_____

Jesus's dear friends summoned him because their brother, another dear friend, was sick. Jesus was slow to move on getting there because he knew this would be an opportunity to grow their faith. But he could see the unbelief all around him when he got there. Jesus broke down in tears. The crowd thought it was because he was sad about his friend Lazarus dying. However, verse 33 tells us Jesus was also angry (or deeply troubled).

Describe what you think Jesus might be angry about.

Jesus may have wept because of the deep grief his friends experienced. Perhaps he wept over their lack of understanding for what he could do. Either way, we see his human emotion. How does it make you feel to know Jesus experienced human emotions?

> The word for *wept* in John 11:31 and the one in verse 33 are not the same verb. In verse 31 it means to weep silently. In verse 33 it means to weep audibly.[*]

What issue are you facing in your life that you need to hear God speak into with similar words to verse 40? How will you reclaim victory there?

> "Groaned in the spirit— Commentators have been much perplexed by the undeniable fact that the Greek word for *groaned* here is expressive of anger rather than grief." Some say, "The Son of man is indignant at the great Enemy, the cause of sorrow and death, with whom he ever struggles, and whom, by dying, he must subdue."[†]

Jesus did this miracle for those standing by just as much as for his dear friends. How does your story benefit "those standing by" and watching God work in your life?

* Marvin Richardson Vincent, *Word Studies in the New Testament*, vol. 2 (New York: Charles Scribner's Sons, 1887), 204–205.

† D. D. Whedon, *Luke–John*, vol. II, *A Popular Commentary on the New Testament* (London: Hodder and Stoughton, 1874), 337.

My prayer to God today is:

_____

_____

_____

_____

MICRO STUDY 3

Read Romans 3:21–25.

Write out Romans 3:24 here:

_____

_____

_____

_____

If you grew up with the idea that you had to be good enough for God to love you, how does this passage affect you?

In what areas of your life do you struggle with accepting God's grace and forgiveness? How does verse 24 speak into that struggle for you?

How will you remind yourself daily that you have been reclaimed and the Enemy has no hold on you?

My prayer to God today is:

_____

_____

_____

MICRO STUDY 4

Read Matthew 7:1–5.

Write out Matthew 7:3 here:

_____

_____

_____

This might be one of the most misconstrued passages in the Bible. It doesn't say to never judge others. But it _does_ tell us to examine our motives and hearts before speaking to someone else about their sin.

How can we discern when it's appropriate to offer constructive criticism or when it is more appropriate to refrain from saying anything?

Jesus illustrated this principle in John 8 with the accusers of the woman caught in adultery. Describe what he said about dealing with personal sin before accusing someone else.

How does remembering that you have been reclaimed from sin help you offer grace to others who are dealing with their sin?

Reflect on how it feels when someone lovingly confronts you in a way that helps you correct your course rather than causing you to feel judged or shamed.

My prayer to God today is:

_____

_____

_____

_____

_____

MICRO STUDY 5

Read Romans 12:1–5.

Write out Romans 12:2 here:

_____

_____

_____

_____

_____

Describe the connection between a renewed mind and worship.

We naturally focus on ourselves, which means we use our bodie to make ourselves happy. When we focus on changing our self-centeredness to a new God-centered focus, then we can worship him. How can God use your renewal to bring glory to him?

The apostle Paul compared the body of Christ to a physical body. How does this help you understand how we are connected and dependent upon other Christians?

My prayer to God today is:

_____

_____

_____

_____

_____

Hope in Action

MAKE TIME THIS WEEK TO REFLECT ON your spiritual journey. Use these prompts to guide your thoughts, or you can create your own based on this lesson. If you're not a fan of journaling, try writing on a whiteboard or chalkboard and then erasing it. You can also download a free printable doodle sheet from the QR code below.

- Praise God, I have been set free from _____.

- Because of Jesus, I now wear the name of _____.

- I am thankful that God's mercy and grace have given me _____.

Look for opportunities to share your story with someone else. Whether it's in a conversation, a short video, or a podcast interview, your story can help someone else feel the power of being reclaimed for Christ.

GET YOUR FREE DOODLE SHEET BY SCANNING THIS CODE WITH YOUR CAMERA

WEEK FIVE
REBIRTH

*And I will give you a new heart, and
I will put a new spirit in you. I will
take out your stony, stubborn heart and
give you a tender, responsive heart.*
—Ezekiel 36:26

First Thoughts

A PIVOTAL MOMENT IS A TIME OR event when everything shifts or turns direction. It is a critical point or a defining moment on which other key events depend. You've had both positive and negative experiences in your life that have defined how you think and react to future events. Some have caused a negative change in your future behavior, and others launched you into even greater things.

Use the journaling lines on this page to reminisce about pivotal moments in your life. The writing prompts below will help you get your thoughts flowing.

What have been the pivotal moments in your life?

What have been the life-changing events?

When do you remember feeling as if a light went on?

What moments felt like a light had been switched off?

What are the moments when you realized something changed the course of events to come?

What milestones mark the steps you've taken to get to where you are now?

_____

_____

_____

_____

_____

_____

_____

STORY

THE PROCESS OF BEING BORN IS AN amazing miracle. Look around at the women in your group, or perhaps the people in the coffee shop where you're sitting, and consider the idea that each started from a single cell called a zygote.* We'll skip explaining how your friend came to be a zygote since that might be too much information for a Bible study—TMI and the age-old where-do-babies-come-from question should be settled already, right? But let's think about the miracle of each person in the room with you.

From her start as a single cell, the friend next to you developed inside her mother's womb, growing fingers and toes, a heart and lungs, a brain, her curly hair, and a freckled nose. Her mother experienced the wonder of carrying a bowling ball around on the front of her body for nine-and-a-half months and trying to sleep with it there.

The science is incredible, but staring into the face of a newborn and wondering how in the world that little creature came out of my body was even more astounding for me. I still can't explain it. To think that every one of us grew inside someone's pelvis for nine months blows my mind!

The birth process itself is difficult to conceive—pun intended. Let's review the short version from an encyclopedia without getting into the brainiac version. There are several stages of labor, with the first being a biochemical change in the infant—yes, the baby starts it all, which should be a clue for things to come—a molecular change that causes the release of hormones that will eventually start uterine contractions. Complex hormonal communication between the mother's body and the baby signals the start of labor. That chemical communication starts weeks before labor and intensifies in the days and hours before active labor begins.[†]

---

* Editors of Encyclopaedia Britannica, "zygote." *Encyclopedia Britannica*, November 21, 2023. https://www.britannica.com/science/zygote.

† A. C. Beck and John W. Huffman, "birth," *Encyclopedia Britannica*, December 12, 2023. https://www.britannica.com/science/birth.

These contractions will cause the shortening and dilation of the cervix, which makes it possible for the baby's melon-sized head to enter the birth canal. The contractions continue and squeeze the baby downward and through the birth canal into the waiting arms of a doctor or a midwife—or an emotional father who has no clue how much his life just changed. The final stage happens after the cord is cut and the placenta is delivered.

It's nearly impossible to fathom how it all works, even after we're holding the eight-pound bundle of joy that emerges from a woman's body. But what if someone told you as an adult that you'd have to go back in and be born again? Is this possible? We are about to study the story of Nicodemus, the man who had to answer this question.

But before we launch into his story, let's think about what it would be like to start life over. Have you ever wished you could go back and start a day over? A year? Your whole life?

What if, instead of having to go back and do it all over again, real life didn't begin until the day you pressed the restart button? You wouldn't have to go back and live it over again, but the best and the most vital part of your life would begin on the day something transformational took place.

God offers a restart through Jesus—a new beginning that makes everything prior feel as if it wasn't living at all.

PRAYER

FATHER, THANK YOU FOR GIVING YOUR ONLY Son, Jesus, so that whoever believes can have eternal life. Thank you for not coming to condemn people but to save us. Open my eyes to the people around me who need to understand what it means to get a fresh start in life. Help me to love generously, living in the love you have shown to me.

I've often heard the saying that God doesn't have grandchildren. The idea is that we aren't born into God's family because of the earthly family we're born into. Being born into a family of Christians doesn't automatically make us a Christian.

EXPLORE THE WORD

ONE OF THE MOST CONFUSING, AND PERHAPS controversial, terms used in some Christian circles is "born again." I encourage you to walk with me into Scripture. Let's set aside pre-existing beliefs about what it might mean, depending on which Christian tradition you grew up in, and explore the Bible. And while we do that, I promise that at the end of this chapter, there will *not* be any challenge to claim "born again" as a title to add to a spiritual pedigree. It's way different from that. You might be surprised to learn that this phrase gained a lot of its popularity in the last 100 years or so, and we don't have to search far into history to find the origins.

As early as the 1920s, some Christian leaders and writers started using the phrase "born-again Christian" to speak of their experiences of converting to Christianity and experiencing a radical life change. However, it was fairly low-key until the fifties and sixties.* The idea came from Scripture, but it really took off as not only a tagline to use but also a way of grouping and sorting Christians.

MEET NICODEMUS

Nicodemus was a Pharisee. Pharisees were the religious leaders who strongly opposed Jesus and his teaching. However, Nicodemus didn't think like all the other Pharisees did. He wanted to know more about Jesus. He was a highly respected and prominent member of the high council—the Sanhedrin. This means he was a zealot for the law and also a purist when it came to religion. Still, Nicodemus's curiosity made him want to know more about Jesus. So he went to see him.

We don't know the reason for the late hour of the visit, yet when John wrote the story in John 3, he felt this was an important detail for us to know—Nicodemus came at night.

---

* Kenneth E. Oritz, "The Birth of the 'Born-Again' Christian," Desiring God website, June 19, 2023, accessed January 30, 2024, https://www.desiringgod.org/articles/the-birth-of-the-born-again-christian.

Have you ever been at a point when you were curious to know more about Jesus, but you didn't want your friends to know? Maybe you checked out church or went to a Bible study, but you didn't want your peers to discover this because you didn't think they would understand.

Describe what it is like to explore your faith in a place where others aren't as receptive (work, home, friendships, etc.).

If you have had days so packed with busyness that you can't seem to find a moment to have a meaningful conversation with God, what prevents you from spending quality time with him?

Why did Nicodemus come at night? We might speculate that he did this because he didn't want his Pharisee friends to know he was seeking Jesus. However, there are other possible reasons. "Rabbis studied and debated long into the night."[*] Or, it might have been that Jesus was overwhelmed by people in the crowds during the day, and this was the first opportunity to have one-on-one time with him.

---

[*] Carson, *The Gospel according to John*, 186.

Nicodemus was a religious man, but he recognized that Jesus was a teacher who did miracles, and he wanted to have a relationship with him. This is a turning point for every one of us—when we realize that religious knowledge, rituals, or traditions are not meaningful if we are missing the relationship with Jesus. Or when we realize we have more questions than answers about our religious traditions. That curiosity is a starting place for new growth.

As you read this story, put yourself in Nicodemus's shoes (maybe sandals?). It's after dark, and you've gone out to find Jesus.

There was a man named Nicodemus, a Jewish religious leader who was a Pharisee. After dark one evening, he came to speak with Jesus. "Rabbi," he said, "we all know that God has sent you to teach us. Your miraculous signs are evidence that God is with you."

Jesus replied, "I tell you the truth, unless you are born again, you cannot see the Kingdom of God."

"What do you mean?" exclaimed Nicodemus. "How can an old man go back into his mother's womb and be born again?"

Jesus replied, "I assure you, no one can enter the Kingdom of God without being born of water and the Spirit. Humans can reproduce only human life, but the Holy Spirit gives birth to spiritual life. So don't be surprised when I say, 'You must be born again.' The wind blows wherever it wants. Just as you can hear the wind but can't tell where it comes from or where it is going, so you can't explain how people are born of the Spirit."

"How are these things possible?" Nicodemus asked. (John 3:1–9)

Nicodemus called Jesus Rabbi—Teacher—and he made a surprising statement: "We all know that God has sent you to teach us. Your miraculous signs are evidence that God is with you."

From what you know about the Pharisees and what we studied in the last chapter, why was this a surprising statement from Nicodemus?

What do you think he meant by "we all know"?

Unlike other Pharisees, who sarcastically called Jesus by the name of *teacher*, Nicodemus didn't have the edge of a sneer in his voice. He said this with respect.

Let's pause to consider that the idea of exploring a path like this is scary, isn't it? Imagine Nicodemus, asking questions when Jesus directly contradicted the legalism of the Pharisees, the very core of everything Nicodemus had followed, likely for years.

What does it feel like when you ask spiritual questions that aren't popular?

What has been your "Nicodemus" experience? Describe your own process of coming to Jesus with your questions.

Nicodemus came under the cover of physical darkness but also in spiritual darkness or blindness. We'll soon see how he stumbled around with trying to understand Jesus. He'd been a rule follower who was familiar with striving and observing microscopic details about adhering to God's commands. And despite all those efforts, he somehow knew that wasn't the way, or he wouldn't have approached Jesus.

Notice how Nicodemus didn't call Jesus the Messiah (v. 2). It appears he fell short of fully understanding Jesus's true identify, yet he saw the miracles as evidence of God's presence in him. As with other encounters, Jesus treated his ignorance with care and respect. He didn't hold the blindness against Nicodemus, but he saw his need. Describe when you have felt as if you were in spiritual darkness.

When have you lived as if strict adherence to religious rules might be the way to earn God's favor?

Born again: "The verb rendered 'to be born' (*gennan*) can refer to the action of the father ('to beget') or the mother ('to give birth to'): the common ingredient is 'generation' or 'regeneration.'" This new birth Jesus talks of, this regeneration, "is *anōthen*, a word that can mean 'from above' or 'again.'"[*]

How did you feel?

BORN AGAIN

Jesus didn't waste time at all with Nicodemus. He got right to telling him he needed to be born again. However, that seemed to confuse Nicodemus. As we already established, it confuses people in our times too.

The term "born again" has taken on some different connotations in our society, mostly because some of the people who claim to have life in Jesus don't always act like followers of Jesus. "Born again" implies a transformation and ongoing process of growing and maturing

---

* Carson, *The Gospel according to John*, 189.

after that spiritual birth. When the evidence of transformation is absent, it turns the label into a contradiction.

This wasn't the first time that Scripture spoke of rebirth and Jesus's role.

> God sent a man, John the Baptist, to tell about the light so that everyone might believe because of his testimony. John himself was not the light; he was simply a witness to tell about the light. The one who is the true light, who gives light to everyone, was coming into the world.
>
> He came into the very world he created, but the world didn't recognize him. He came to his own people, and even they rejected him. But to all who believed him and accepted him, he gave the right to become children of God. They are reborn—not with a physical birth resulting from human passion or plan, but a birth that comes from God.
>
> So the Word became human and made his home among us. He was full of unfailing love and faithfulness. And we have seen his glory, the glory of the Father's one and only Son. (John 1:6–14)

"'Word' translates the Greek *logos*, a term Greeks used not only of the spoken word but also of the unspoken word—the reason. When they applied it to the universe, they meant the rational principle that governs all things. The Jews, however, used it to refer to the 'word' of God by which he created the world and governs it."[*]

---

[*] *NIV Study Bible*, (Grand Rapids: Zondervan 1985, 1995, 2002, 2008, 2011).

Notice again here the contrast of light and how it ties in with spiritual birth. In this passage, Jesus is "the Word." Other places in Scripture talk about being dead in our sins, comparing the darkness with a grave (Ephesians 2:1–6; Colossians 2:13; Romans 6:4–6). In this way, the regeneration spoken of in some places as rebirth is like a resurrection from death in sin.

How does the picture of being spiritually dead and then given a new chance at life resonate with you?

When Jesus told Nicodemus he needed to be born again, he offered a restart. But Nicodemus acted as if Jesus were suggesting that he return to his mother's womb and come out again. We don't know whether he truly didn't understand what Jesus meant or if he was being intentionally thickheaded. As a teacher of the law and a person who had studied it, Nicodemus would know what the Scripture said. So, Jesus challenged him.

> Jesus replied, "You are a respected Jewish teacher, and yet you don't understand these things? I assure you, we tell you what we know and have seen, and yet you won't believe our testimony. But if you don't believe me when I tell you about earthly things, how can you possibly believe if I tell you about heavenly things? No one has ever gone to heaven and returned. But the Son of Man has come down from heaven." (John 3:10–13)

Nicodemus, as an expert in Scripture, would have known these promises from the Old Testament that speak to the ways God renews:

> "But this is the new covenant I will make with the people of Israel after those days," says the LORD. "I will put my instructions deep within them, and I will write them on their hearts. I will be their God, and they will be my people. And they will not need to teach their neighbors, nor will they need to teach their relatives, saying, 'You should know the LORD.' For everyone, from the least to

the greatest, will know me already," says the LORD. "And
I will forgive their wickedness, and I will never again remember their sins." (Jeremiah 31:33–34)

And I will give you a new heart, and I will put a new
spirit in you. I will take out your stony, stubborn heart
and give you a tender, responsive heart. And I will put
my Spirit in you so that you will follow my decrees and
be careful to obey my regulations ... You will be my people, and I will be your God. (Ezekiel 36:26–28)

List your observations about these two passages and what kind of
rebirth they represent.

Being "born again" is not a label we slap on. It means having a new
heart and a new attitude. It includes belonging to God as a son or
a daughter, just as if we had been born physically of a parent. Being
born again is not about living a good moral life, being a good person,
or following rules. It's about having a relationship with God, having
his Holy Spirit living inside of you.

    We now come to one of the most quoted verses in the Bible. But
as we study it in context, you'll see it's so much more than one verse.

"And as Moses lifted up the bronze snake on a pole in
the wilderness, so the Son of Man must be lifted up, so
that everyone who believes in him will have eternal life.

I could *call* myself a speed runner, but if you discovered I'd only sprinted from a hideous spider once, would you still consider me a runner? Would I be equipped to coach others? Nope. Arachnophobia doesn't make me an athlete.

Similarly, saying a quick prayer and going back to whatever we were before is not what it means to be born again. Rebirth doesn't come from applying a label to an altar call.

"For this is how God loved the world: He gave his one and only Son, so that everyone who believes in him will not perish but have eternal life. God sent his Son into the world not to judge the world, but to save the world through him.

"There is no judgment against anyone who believes in him. But anyone who does not believe in him has already been judged for not believing in God's one and only Son. And the judgment is based on this fact: God's light came into the world, but people loved the darkness more than the light, for their actions were evil. All who do evil hate the light and refuse to go near it for fear their sins will be exposed. But those who do what is right come to the light so others can see that they are doing what God wants." (John 3:14–21)

Whoever believes in Jesus has new life, a rebirth. Imagine how Nicodemus might have felt when hearing about a gift for everyone who believed, not something exclusive to people who adhered to laws, rules, and regulations. Imagine hearing of love instead of wrath.

When did you first realize how much God loves you?

How has this been a transformation or a rebirth for you?

Perhaps you don't often hear John 3:16 along with verses 17 and 18. What comes to mind for you when you think of Jesus not coming to condemn the world?

The process of being born brings a baby from darkness to instant light. What does it mean to move from spiritual darkness into light?

"Is there a single one of us rulers or Pharisees who believes in him? This foolish crowd follows him, but they are ignorant of the law. God's curse is on them!"

Then Nicodemus, the leader who had met with Jesus earlier, spoke up. "Is it legal to convict a man before he is given a hearing?" he asked.

They replied, "Are you from Galilee, too? Search the Scriptures and see for yourself—no prophet ever comes from Galilee!" (John 7:48–52)

We don't know what happened to Nicodemus at this moment. Unlike the apostle Paul, who had a dramatic and instant change, we don't see that here with Nicodemus. We don't see evidence he said anything indicating that he became a follower of Christ right then. But we do see a few glimpses of him in two other places in John. He appeared again in John 7 when he was part of a high council meeting of the Pharisees and leading priests. He spoke up to point out that the Pharisees were disregarding the law in their supposed observance of the law, and he called for a fair trial for Jesus.

Some of the Pharisees did believe in Jesus, but there was such peer pressure and mockery from those who didn't believe. Imagine being in Nicodemus's shoes, trying to defend Jesus! These leaders wanted to kill Jesus, so admitting to following him would be a dangerous thing.

The last time Nicodemus appears in the Bible is right after Jesus's death in John 19:39. He brought expensive spices to anoint Jesus's body for burial—the kind of spices that would be used for royalty. By doing this, he took a public stand with Jesus.

KNOWING THE TRUTH

There are several things we can learn from Nicodemus's story. Imagine being in his position: knowing the truth but feeling trapped by your peers and circumstances. Based on what we do see of him after his nighttime encounter with Jesus, deep in his heart, he desired to follow Jesus.

In addition to being physically born to our parents, each of us also needs to come to a moment in life when we realize that we need to be spiritually born. When I say moment, I mean that it might come gradually. Rebirth doesn't have to happen like a bolt of lightning with an altar call. Rebirth comes when we get to the end of all the striving and realize we can't call ourselves God's family by being a good person or following the Ten Commandments. Going to church, getting confirmed, or being religious isn't the way either. It's acknowledging that Jesus is the only way and starting over.

Another lesson we can draw from Nicodemus's story is that we are never truly alone in our faith. In our daily lives, we might sometimes feel isolated in our faith. But there are others, like Nicodemus, who share our beliefs but haven't spoken up about their faith in Jesus. This realization can bring us comfort and a sense of connection in our spiritual journey.

We don't know how Nicodemus responded after meeting with Jesus the first time, but when he appeared again in John 7, some change had started, and by the time we see him in John 19, it's clear that he was a bold believer in Jesus. Nicodemus was reborn.

Some might say that Nicodemus's decision to take his stand after Jesus's death was too late. But that isn't true. God works on each of us in his own timing. It is never too late to make a change and start over.

NEVER TOO LATE

There is no shame or embarrassment in admitting you've gone to church your whole life but have never publicly made a declaration of belief in Jesus. It isn't too late to do it. It isn't too late for someone you know to change either. God works on our hearts in different ways. We will never understand why one person immediately gives their life to Christ when another isn't ready, even after many encounters with Jesus.

Jesus said, "The wind blows wherever it wants. Just as you can hear the wind but can't tell where it comes from or where it is going, so you can't explain how people are born of the Spirit" (John 3:8). There is some mystery in it all, but the Holy Spirit is at work, even when we can't see anything happening.

What part of God's work in your life feels mysterious, as if you can't put it into words?

Ultimately, Jesus challenged Nicodemus's identity. His commitment to religious activities, study, and piety would no longer be the core of his reputation. The Pharisees loved to condemn people, but Jesus came in love, not to condemn people but to save them.

Jesus spoke directly to Nicodemus's need. He told him what he needed to hear—not fake words that would appease him and make him feel better but clear truth about what could change his life. Imagine also what a relief it might have been for Nicodemus to hear that Jesus's work would replace his feeble attempts toward perfection.

What does it mean to you when you think of Jesus replacing your striving and exchanging it for grace?

God's Word speaks clearly to us and tells us we can be reborn and experience new life too. If you've been trying to follow the rules and be a good person, Jesus offers you the same as he did to Nicodemus: believe. This belief goes beyond acknowledging Jesus as a great teacher who did miraculous things. This is recognizing that Jesus is the Son of God who was crucified to rebirth us into eternal life with him after our physical bodies die.

So, we see that "born again" isn't a label, a box to check on a survey, or a moment we mark on a bracelet. It's the process Jesus brings us through as we pass from simple belief into a brand-new life. After that rebirth, we begin to grow and mature, and people might start to notice how much we resemble our heavenly Father. Instead of a title, it's a way of life.

> Once we, too, were foolish and disobedient. We were misled and became slaves to many lusts and pleasures. Our lives were full of evil and envy, and we hated each other. But—When God our Savior revealed his kindness and love, he saved us, not because of the righteous things we had done, but because of his mercy. He washed away our sins, giving us a new birth and new life through the Holy Spirit. He generously poured out the Spirit upon us through Jesus Christ our Savior. Because of his grace he made us right in his sight and gave us confidence that we will inherit eternal life. (Titus 3:3–7)

Prayer Journal

I'M THANKFUL FOR:

_____

_____

_____

_____

_____

_____

I'M ASKING GOD FOR:

_____

_____

_____

_____

_____

_____

WORDS OF WORSHIP TO GOD:

_____

_____

_____

_____

_____

_____

APPLY

MICRO STUDY 1

Read 1 Peter 1:1–5, 21–25

Write out 1 Peter 1:3 here:

_____

_____

_____

_____

_____

_____

In this passage, Peter talks about being born again to a living hope through the resurrection of Jesus Christ from the dead. What does this living hope mean to you personally?

How does the fact that we are born again into an inheritance that is kept in heaven for us (v. 4) impact how we live our lives here on earth?

As God continues transforming your thinking, how have you seen it affect your relationships in your family, workplace, and community?

My prayer to God today is:

_____

_____

_____

_____

_____

MICRO STUDY 2

Read 1 John 3:1–7.

Write out the second half of 1 John 3:7 here:

_____

_____

_____

How does the assurance of your identity as a child of God give you hope and confidence as you navigate the challenges and uncertainties of life?

Where has God challenged you the most when it comes to living like Jesus?

This passage identifies love as the primary evidence of our family affiliation with Jesus. Why do you think love is the primary evidence?

Describe what this kind of love looks like in action.

My prayer to God today is:

_____

_____

_____

_____

_____

MICRO STUDY 3

Read John 14:23–31.

Write out John 14:27 here:

_____

_____

_____

_____

Moments before, Jesus had explained that he would soon be betrayed and arrested (John 13). Earlier in chapter 14, he assured his disciples that he would not abandon them as orphans when he died (v. 18). He would return. And he would leave them with the Holy Spirit as an ever-present Advocate. As members of God's family, he also had a gift for them.

Describe what the gift in verse 27 means for someone reborn into God's family versus the kind of peace the world offers.

How have you experienced Jesus's peace amid your challenges and uncertainties?

> This peace is similar to _shalom_, the Jewish word for greeting and farewell. And the "verb (_aphienai_) probably here has the sense of 'bequeaths.'"[*]

What are the things that most threaten your personal peace?

_____

[*] Carson, _The Gospel according to John_, 505.

Jesus gives his peace in the same sense of the word *bequeath*—as in willing something to someone or passing it down. When you realize that Jesus transferred ownership of his peace to you, how does it speak to the threats you experience?

My prayer to God today is:

_____

_____

_____

_____

_____

MICRO STUDY 4

Read Ephesians 4:17–32.

Write out Ephesians 4:23–24 here:

_____

_____

_____

_____

_____

When we are reborn into God's family, he gives us new spiritual clothing. It's as if we arrived with nothing but a trash bag of ratty clothes, and he then exchanges them for something brand new.

When you see the list in this passage, which can you identify as part of your old "clothing" before Christ?

How does Paul describe the difference between living apart from God and being in his family?

What does it mean to let the Spirit renew your thoughts and attitudes (v. 23)? What has he completely transformed in you?

Verse 30 says he has identified you as his own! Describe how it feels to be God's "own."

How do you renew your mind daily?

My prayer to God today is:

_____

_____

_____

_____

_____

MICRO STUDY 5

Read Colossians 3:5–14.

Write out Colossians 3:12–14 here:

_____

_____

_____

_____

_____

_____

_____

What similarities do you see here in this passage and in yesterday's study from Ephesians?

Reflect on your transformation process as you seek to align your life with the values and virtues outlined in this passage. In what areas do you see growth, and where do you still need to surrender to God's transforming work?

How does being born into God's family through faith in Jesus Christ impact how we live and interact with others, as described in these verses?

Verse 10 talks about being renewed as we learn to know our Creator. How does knowing God more deeply transform your thoughts, attitudes, and actions?

My prayer to God today is:

_____

_____

_____

_____

_____

Hope in Action

IF YOU FEEL COMFORTABLE SHARING, TELL SOMEONE else about one of the pivotal moments you wrote about at the beginning of this lesson. As you share, use these cues to help you format your story into something that helps others see the transformation in ways they might relate to:

- What made this a pivotal moment for you?
- What would you do differently now that you know more?
- How has Jesus changed and renewed hurts and struggles?
- How have you learned to recognize Jesus's voice better?
- When have you felt alone, like Nicodemus, where you weren't ready for other people to know you wanted to get to know Jesus more?
- How did you overcome that fear and let others in on what Jesus was doing in your life?
- How have you changed and grown over time?

It's important to remember that we look back not to dwell on the pain but to promote healing. We also don't want to minimize it by skipping over the trauma. Now that you've thought about it, is there someone you haven't yet forgiven for their role in a negative turning point in your life?

If one of the pivotal moments you wrote about is a positive one, have you expressed your gratitude to the people who were part of that event? Consider telling someone how much it still means to you that they were part of this life-changing experience.

WEEK SIX
REMAIN

*I am the vine; you are the branches.
Those who remain in me, and I in
them, will produce much fruit. For
apart from me you can do nothing.*
—John 15:5

First Thoughts

DRAW IMAGES OR WORDS ON BRANCHES OF the vine, describing the kinds of fruit you have seen grow in your life (representing your spiritual life and actions). Include spiritual milestones and qualities that have grown.

STORY

MY GRANDFATHER WAS A CAREFUL GARDENER WHO tended the flowers, trees, and fruit in his large yard. He spent his summers hoeing, weeding, and pruning, and tanning his olive skin during hours bent over or kneeling between rows. As he harvested the tomatoes, green beans, peaches, and pears, my grandmother filled canning jars and stocked the cellar shelves.

Among the cherry trees and vegetables were rows of the most beautiful and fragrant roses. The summer I turned fifteen, I traveled to Washington State to spend two weeks with my grandparents. During that stay, Grandpa invited me to keep a vase on my nightstand supplied with massive, fresh-cut tea rose blooms. The aroma filled my room. I learned that once we snipped a rose off the vine, it would flourish for only a short time before its beauty faded and the petals dropped off.

On our sporadic visits to the Pacific Northwest, I loved wandering garden paths with Grandpa, watching his careful clipping of vines and branches, learning which were weeds and which were plants. His passion for teaching—he was a retired school principal—showed up in the garden as he passed years of wisdom to me with lessons that often began with, "Honey, look at this."

REALITY CHECK

Before this gets too nostalgic or charming, it would be helpful to insert some transparency here. I appreciated his example, but I have not upheld the standards well. I love growing things and getting my hands into the soil. Perennials are a fixture in the flowerbeds adorning my front yard.

But my own flower garden would never bring beaming looks of pride from Grandpa if he were still alive today. It's more of a chaotic carnival of unruly flora—one where the flowers engage in a colorful dance of disobedience and the weeds throw a lively party in the gaps between the paving stones.

It's a botanical revolt, where there is just enough semblance of order to look pretty from the road. Just don't walk up the pathway to the door. Those white flowers that insist on being the headlining act are weeds. And those morning glories showed up one day uninvited. I just let them be. I forgot to prune the hydrangea bush, so pardon how its blossoms kiss the ground this year. I'll get to them next year. I think. I let the apples go to the deer because I couldn't reach half of them—due to a lack of good pruning.

Pruning has a purpose. I've seen how my raspberry bushes have become tangled in their competition for sunlight. Finding the fruit among the overgrown vines and dead branches is also nearly impossible. Last season, I gave the blueberries some attention, and we enjoyed an amazing crop of daily goodness for a month!

ROOTED FOR A PURPOSE

When I planted those blueberry bushes, I set out to grow fruit. I didn't plant them for their leaves or stems. Even though those parts of the plant are vital to its health and stability, the point was fruit. I wanted blueberries to bake into pies and muffins, to sit on my back porch savoring them straight off the vine with some whipped cream on top. But for the first few years, they never blossomed or produced berries. Then I learned that I needed to plant diverse varieties before they could cross-pollinate into bushes that yielded fruit. There's another metaphor there that I'll save for another time.

This week, we're looking at what it means to remain in Jesus, the Vine, to bear fruit. We'll also explore the process of spiritual pruning. In the plant world, pruning is a meticulous process. It isn't like when the power company comes with a big brush machine with spinning blades and shreds all the vegetation under our lines, leaving a mess of ragged and sheared branches behind. Pruning is a careful selection of removing what hinders the plant's growth.

Likewise, spiritual pruning isn't God mowing us down without mercy. In the gentle hands of the Gardener, it becomes a careful and intentional sculpting of our souls rather than an act of ruthless eradication. As God, the skilled and loving horticulturist, trims away the excess, we discover how to flourish for the authentic purpose to which he calls us.

PRAYER

FATHER, I ASK YOU TO OPEN MY heart to perceive the truth we are about to study. Let the words take root and nurture a deeper understanding of my connection to you as the Vine and the importance of abiding in your love. Give me the humility to receive pruning so that I can produce fruit that has the qualities of your Spirit.

EXPLORE THE WORD

BEFORE WE EXPLORE JOHN 15, LET'S LOOK at where this chapter falls in the progression of Jesus's earthly life before his crucifixion. The disciples had already had their Passover meal (what we refer to as the Last Supper) with Jesus, where he washed their feet, broke bread, and predicted that Judas would betray him and Peter would deny him (John 13). Sometimes, I get thrown off by the fact that the Bible has chapter divisions in the middle of a scene. In the book of John, chapters 14 to 17 are all part of what Jesus said to his disciples after supper. Think of it as his farewell message to them.

In chapter 14, he spoke of how he would be leaving but that the Father would send the Comforter, the Holy Spirit. He offered words of assurance for the uncertainty that was about to come. "'I am leaving you with a gift—peace of mind and heart. And the peace I give is a gift the world cannot give. So don't be troubled or afraid. Remember what I told you: I am going away, but I will come back to you again'" (John 14:27–28).

Chapter 14 ended with Jesus saying, "Let's be going," and it's unclear from John's writing if they left the upper room and went for a walk together or if he continued speaking there. However, the Gospel of Matthew gives some clues. Here is what happened after they ate.

Then they sang a hymn and went out to the Mount of Olives.

On the way, Jesus told them, "Tonight all of you will desert me. For the Scriptures say, 'God will strike the Shepherd, and the sheep of the flock will be scattered.'

But after I have been raised from the dead, I will go ahead of you to Galilee and meet you there." (Matthew 26:30–32)

After this, Matthew said, Jesus had a discussion with Peter about how the disciple would deny Jesus. And then, Jesus went to pray in the olive grove called Gethsemane. We know that this all happened on the day before Jesus was crucified, the same evening, and hours before he was arrested. So, as we look at John 15, let's remember that context.

VINE AND BRANCHES

This isn't the only place where a parable included a reference to vines or vineyards. See also: Matthew 20:1–16; Matthew 21:28–41; Mark 12:1–9; Luke 13:6–9; Luke 20:9–16.

"I am the true grapevine, and my Father is the gardener. He cuts off every branch of mine that doesn't produce fruit, and he prunes the branches that do bear fruit so they will produce even more. You have already been pruned and purified by the message I have given you. Remain in me, and I will remain in you. For a branch cannot produce fruit if it is severed from the vine, and you cannot be fruitful unless you remain in me." (John 15:1–4)

Now that you've heard some of the backstory before this passage begins, what thoughts come to mind about remaining in Jesus?

Luke 22:24 says that the disciples started arguing among themselves right there at the Last Supper, right after Jesus broke bread and poured wine, about who would be the greatest among them. Imagine, then, what it must have been like to consider pruning regarding the attitudes Jesus saw them display. Part of Jesus's long conversation with his disciples was predicting how difficult it would be for them to remain true to his teaching in the days that were about to come.

If the disciples fought among themselves, how might that have made it more difficult to persevere in faith?

"Within Jewish tradition, the vine was a picture of Israel. God brought a vine out of Egypt, and planted it in the promised land (Psalm 80:8–18)," N. T. Wright said. "It had been ravaged by wild animals and needed protecting and re-establishing. The vineyard of Israel, said Isaiah in chapter 5, has borne wild grapes instead of proper ones. Other prophets used the same picture." [**]

How important was their solidarity in the face of persecution and difficulty?

[**] N. T. (Tom) Wright, *John for Everyone, Part 2: Chapters 11-21* (London: Society for Promoting Christian Knowledge, 2004), 70.

That solidarity (sometimes called fellowship) with one another was synonymous with remaining in Jesus because of his repeated command to love each other. We'll look at that shortly. As you look at verses 1–4, notice that Jesus is the vine, and the Father is the gardener. The gardener "owns the vine, tends the vine, prunes the vine, seeks its fruit and is glorified in its fruitfulness."[*] The vine sustains the branches, but the *branches* bear the fruit. The more fruit they bear, the more glory they bring to the Father.

The concept of remaining goes all the way back to the Old Testament when God promised the people of Israel that he would

---

[*] Dongell, *John*, 181.

"walk among" them. "I will be your God, and you will be my people" (Leviticus 26:12). But now we have Jesus, who lived among us as a human, as our way of connecting to the Father.

FRUIT AND ABIDING

> "Yes, I am the vine; you are the branches. Those who remain in me, and I in them, will produce much fruit. For apart from me you can do nothing. Anyone who does not remain in me is thrown away like a useless branch and withers. Such branches are gathered into a pile to be burned. But if you remain in me and my words remain in you, you may ask for anything you want, and it will be granted! When you produce much fruit, you are my true disciples. This brings great glory to my Father." (John 15:5–8)

Because this fruit matters, the Gardener cuts off the branches that don't bear any fruit, the ones that are no longer connected to Christ because they no longer abide. Jesus had become the Father's instrument by which the fruit would appear. The pruning happened on the branches that had fruit to make them even more fruitful.

Think of it this way: When I prune my fruit bushes, I first remove all the dead stems. Once I can see the space, then I begin trimming the living branches to get them to the healthiest point for the future harvest.

When have you tried to produce spiritual "fruit" without Jesus?

James Bryan Smith defines abiding (remaining) in Christ this way: "To abide means to rest and rely on Jesus, who is not outside of us, judging us, but inside of us, empowering us. The more deeply we are aware of our identity in Christ, and of his presence and power that are with us, the more naturally we will do this."*

---

*James Bryan Smith, *The Good and Beautiful God* (Downers Grove, Ill.: InterVarsity Press, 2009), p. 159.

A branch that loses its connection with Jesus becomes lifeless. Can you recall a time when you felt spiritually withered?

What comfort and strength do you receive from where it speaks in these verses of a mutual abiding (Jesus in us and us in him)?

For a long time, I understood this metaphor to be a picture of the branches that bore fruit (good Christians) versus those that didn't produce anything Christlike (people who weren't "good" Christians). *Other* people with problems and surely not me! But now I see this was a prideful way of puffing up my goodness and missing the point. Jesus was talking about pruning *my* deadness, all the places where I produce none of the qualities he wants in me. When Jesus gets out his pruners, it's for believers too—a continual process, not one time.

Jesus did not coerce his disciples to remain in a relationship with him. Judas freely made the decision to pursue his own way. Judas would show his absence of fruit within hours of the meal he shared with Jesus. But Jesus's instructions carried more weight than these disciples could understand. They didn't have any idea of what would happen in the next few days. So, there he was with eleven. And he gave them one command: remain.

If they did, they would see fruit. But what does it look like? What is the fruit God looks for in his disciples? Love. That's what God the Father wants to see in the harvest that will bring glory to his name.

"I have loved you even as the Father has loved me. Remain in my love. When you obey my commandments, you remain in my love, just as I obey my Father's commandments and remain in his love. I have told you these things so that you will be filled with my joy. Yes, your joy will overflow!

This is my commandment: Love each other in the same way I have loved you. There is no greater love than to lay down one's life for one's friends. You are my friends if you do what I command. I no longer call you slaves, because a master doesn't confide in his slaves. Now you are my friends, since I have told you everything the Father told me. You didn't choose me. I chose you.

I appointed you to go and produce lasting fruit, so that the Father will give you whatever you ask for, using my name. This is my command: Love each other." (John 15:9–17)

Does the simplicity surprise you? Why or why not?

In the passage above, underline what Jesus promises those who remain in this love. Which of these promises have you experienced in your life?

Describe the role of obedience in what Jesus said.

How would you describe "lasting fruit"?

Jesus called them his friends three times here! In the passage right after this, he went on to explain how the world would persecute them because it persecuted him. As his friends, they would experience the same hostility. This was why they needed to remain. It would be difficult to obey amid persecution and rejection.

How does the vine and branches metaphor help you understand the relationship between Jesus and believers?

At the end of John 15, Jesus promised again (the same as he did in chapter 14) that the Comforter, the Holy Spirit, would be coming. In the NLT, this is translated as the "Advocate—the Spirit of truth." The Spirit helps us produce the fruit that the Father wants to see.

THE SIMPLICITY OF REMAINING

Perhaps you have heard complicated explanations of the gospel, followed by even more complicated steps of what it means to be a follower of Christ. But Jesus gave three simple steps:

Believe.

Remain.

Produce fruit.

I've spent years teaching complex versions of discipleship, giving people to-do lists, tasks, and goals. But while writing this book, Jesus has challenged me to strip away the Pharisaical rules and tasks that still persisted in my understanding of what discipleship means. He has pruned and continues to trim away some dead habits.

Describe what you think each of these means:

Believe –

Remain –

Produce fruit –

We will return to these ideas in a moment. First, let's take another look at the fruit Jesus looks for in us.

THE QUALITIES OF LASTING FRUIT

In his letter to the Galatians, the apostle Paul talked about how the Holy Spirit guides and gives the desires stand up against sin. He also made it clear that being directed by the Spirit did not mean going back to following the law of Moses (Galatians 5:16–18). He listed examples of sinful desires and then contrasted those with the fruit the Spirit produces.

> But the Holy Spirit produces this kind of fruit in our lives: love, joy, peace, patience, kindness, goodness, faithfulness, gentleness, and self-control. There is no law against these things!
>
> Those who belong to Christ Jesus have nailed the passions and desires of their sinful nature to his cross and crucified them there. Since we are living by the Spirit, let us follow the Spirit's leading in every part of our lives. Let us not become conceited, or provoke one another, or be jealous of one another. (Galatians 5:22–26)

I often notice that people refer to this as the "fruits of the Spirit," with an emphasis on the plural fruits. But when I look at the verse in multiple translations of the Bible, most of them include this phrase: the fruit of the Spirit *is*." It doesn't say they *are*. Notice it says "this kind of fruit" rather than these kinds of fruit above.

If we think of these as individual fruits, as if the Holy Spirit is making some sort of fruit salad in us, then we might make excuses when we feel as if we've run out of one. We might dismiss gentleness or patience, thinking we have enough kindness or love to make up for it. However, these are all qualities of the fruit we need to produce. Rather than a fruit salad where we can put in a little of each in different quantities, what if God wants our fruit to have all these qualities. If the main fruit is love, then it must be joyful, peaceful, patient, kind, good, faithful, gentle, and self-controlled. Love is *all* of those things.

Let's use a peach as an example. The peach is the fruit, but it must be all of these things to be pleasing: juicy, sweet, tender, aromatic, flavorful, fresh, beautiful, and velvety. Which characteristic would you eliminate? If it weren't sweet or flavorful, you'd spit it out, right?

What comes to mind when you think of the fruit of the Spirit as the qualities God wants to develop in you?

Read the following passage and then underline the similarities with Galatians 5.

> Love is patient and kind. Love is not jealous or boastful or proud or rude. It does not demand its own way. It is not irritable, and it keeps no record of being wronged. It does not rejoice about injustice but rejoices whenever the truth wins out. Love never gives up, never loses faith, is always hopeful, and endures through every circumstance. (1 Corinthians 13:4–7)

When you have read the characteristics of the fruit of the Spirit in the past, would you say you typically think of them as things you need to work on or as what God produces in you?

For much of my life, I mistakenly believed I had to strive to be a better person to earn God's love. As if God would somehow love me more if I figured out how to do life perfectly. But this is backward. Fruit is the result of growth, not the other way around. And how to we grow? As John 15 teaches, the answer is simple: remain.

Pause for a moment to absorb that. What thoughts come to mind?

Imagine this prayer: "Lord, produce love in me. Amen." Children attending Sunday services might be delighted if the deacon or pastor traded the usual fifteen-minute monotone congregational prayer for a simple one: Lord, produce love in me. They could hardly fidget through that one!

The simple truth is that if we prayed for love, the other parts would follow. The act of praying is part of "remaining in," vitally connected to Jesus, our Vine.

Look at 1 Corinthians 13:4–7 above again. List the qualities that would result in the fruit of love:

> The Greek word *menō* is a verb that means "remain, stay (i.e., lodge) with" and can "refer to *dwelling, living, or lodging.* Similar to English 'stay,' *menō* is sometimes used as a simple expression for dwelling in an abode or sharing quarters."[*]

What distracts you right now from remaining in Jesus, pulls you away from his power and life-giving love?

[*] Garwood P. Anderson, "Hospitality," in *Lexham Theological Wordbook*, ed. Douglas Mangum et al., Lexham Bible Reference Series (Bellingham, WA: Lexham Press, 2014).

Remaining in Jesus is how we experience flourishing life. It might be tempting to create an action plan that includes *doing* more. It might look something like this: set my alarm for 5:00 a.m. to prayer and read my Bible, pray instead of scrolling social media, go to church every week, get more Christian friends, start a gratitude journal, memorize Scripture, and buy a new spiritual goals planner.

Stop.

There isn't a to-do list for abiding or remaining. Although those things aren't bad, this is about a relationship where we make him at home in us and we make him our home. At home, we talk throughout the day; we *live* together. We cling to him and desperately need him. We listen to one another. Notice how the to-do list puts it all in our own power to accomplish the tasks. Instead, this is about our constant awareness that he is with us when we eat, sleep, converse with others, breathe. The branches flow right into the Vine.

RETHINKING MOTIVES

So many of the habits we think of today as ones that help us remain are related to literacy. Most of Jesus's disciples didn't read! And none of them had a personal Bible with little boxed devotions for each day. They learned to listen to the Word and then go about daily life, flourishing on the Vine.

I saw a social media post from someone who had been wounded by her church. She showed a picture of a flower that bloomed on her sidewalk after she'd snipped it off. To her, it was evidence that what she'd been taught about John 15 wasn't true, that she didn't need to remain in Jesus at all. "I can still bloom on my own," she said.

Somehow, she hadn't thought a few days ahead—to when that blossom would be nothing but dead, trampled petals with no sustaining life in them. We *do* need Jesus. Love on its own is brief and fading. It chokes when real hardship tests it. She had confounded Jesus with the church that wounded her. I'm empathetic to how it happened. Abuse and the trauma that grew from it made her believe *that* was the result of remaining in Jesus. However, that was a weed that tried to choke out the Vine.

Remaining in Jesus is not a list of things to do. Any habits or practices that we apply must first have sprouted from remaining and abiding. Apart from Jesus, no spiritual habit will change our hearts. No love will grow.

Write a sentence that describes this remaining and abiding in your own words.

If you grew up believing that doing things for God was supposed to be evidence of abiding, what have you learned about striving from this lesson?

James Bryan Smith said, "The focus should be on the relationship, not the rules. Our Christian lives are in real trouble when we focus mainly on rule keeping. We must remain focused on our identity in Christ and let that determine our behavior. When I know and reflect on the reality that Christ dwells in me, my desire to nurture that relationship strengthens."[*]

---

[*] Smith, *The Good and Beautiful Life*, 209.

Being with other Christians in a relationship at a church is helpful. So is reading our Bibles. But for my entire life, I was taught that if I cut myself off from those things, I would wither up and die spiritually. There was a heavy emphasis on being fulfilled by the church first instead of the other way around—fulfilled by Jesus to flourish in community. When I studied what it means to dwell and remain in Jesus, it opened my eyes to how much I was hoping to find spiritual life in humans who were as spiritually malnourished as I was.

"Apart from me you can do nothing," Jesus said (John 15:5). Above all, what withers us spiritually is being cut off from the Vine. If we aren't remaining in Jesus, we're just dead branches trying to find life in other branches instead of the Vine. What a tangled mess that is!

Of course, we need others. But first, we need Jesus. Without him, we have no orchard. No vineyard. No rose garden.

A bouquet of synthetic flowers *looks* similar to thriving foliage and blooms. Similarly, a bowl of artificial apples and oranges appears legitimate at first. But up close, it is cheap and plasticky.

Jesus calls us not to look like him but to *be* like him. That comes through a life-giving connection to him.

Life in God's garden is beautiful and messy and hard. But love, the defining fruit of our life in Christ, is sweeter than anything we can imagine. Stay with Jesus, taped and tied as a grafted branch that depends on the Vine for everything. Talk with Jesus. Study God's Word. But instead of obsessing about whether you're doing enough, fuse yourself to Jesus above all, and you'll never wonder if your effort was enough. You'll find unlimited refreshment when you remain in him.

Prayer Journal

I'M THANKFUL FOR:

_____

_____

_____

_____

_____

_____

I'M ASKING GOD FOR:

_____

_____

_____

_____

_____

_____

WORDS OF WORSHIP TO GOD:

_____

_____

_____

_____

_____

_____

APPLY

MICRO STUDY 1

Read Hebrews 10:15–25.

Write out Hebrews 10:23 here:

_____

_____

_____

_____

_____

What comes to mind when you think of words like *hold tightly* or *unwavering?*

What daily practices help you remember to abide in Christ and remain steadfast in your faith?

We have no barrier between us and God. We can communicate with him at any time, and he knows our needs. How does that comfort you as you follow Jesus's instruction to remain in him (John 15)?

How does meeting with other Christians help you remain connected to Jesus?

My prayer to God today is:

_____

_____

_____

_____

_____

MICRO STUDY 2

Read Psalm 51.

Write out Psalm 51:10 here:

_____

_____

_____

King David, the author of this psalm, knew what it was like to disappoint God. Simon Peter was familiar with this kind of disappointment too. He said he would be loyal to Jesus to death (John 13), but when the heat turned up, he pretended not to know Jesus (John 18). Jesus gave him another chance in John 21—after the resurrection—to pledge his love to Christ again.

We will mess up. We're human. But remaining in Jesus is possible through confessing and repenting (turning the other way) from our sin.

In the first part of Psalm 51, David asked for God's mercy and forgiveness. How does this concept of relying on God's grace for forgiveness apply to your own life?

David used the word *restore* (v. 12). What has restoration looked like in your life?

In verse 10, David asked for a clean heart and renewed loyalty. This is what it means to abide in Jesus too. Describe how it feels to be restored in your relationship with Jesus when you've strayed.

My prayer to God today is:

_____

_____

_____

_____

_____

MICRO STUDY 3

Read Romans 5:1–5.

Write out Romans 5:1 here:

_____

_____

_____

_____

_____

When you think of being "made right" in God's eyes, what thoughts come to mind?

How does it affect your desire to want to remain connected to Jesus when you realize the magnitude of what he has done for you?

What does it mean to rejoice about running into problems?

How have you seen endurance, strength, character, and hope grow in your life as you trust in God?

My prayer to God today is:

_____

_____

_____

_____

_____

MICRO STUDY 4

Read Romans 5:6–11.

Write out Romans 5:11 here:

_____

_____

_____

_____

How does Jesus's act of sacrifice challenge and inspire you in your own relationships and love toward others?

Verse 11 speaks of the joy we have in God through Jesus Christ. How does the assurance of being made right with God bring joy and peace to your life, especially in difficult times?

How can you practically apply the truths found in these verses to your relationships with others, both within and outside the church community?

How does understanding and accepting God's love, demonstrated through Christ's sacrifice, impact your ability to love and forgive others who may have wronged you?

My prayer to God today is:

_____

_____

_____

_____

_____

MICRO STUDY 5

Read Luke 4:14–22.

Write out Luke 4: 18–19 here:

_____

_____

_____

_____

_____

_____

_____

Now that we've seen what it means to be refreshed by an encounter with Jesus, all of these examples from John certainly underscore Jesus's word here in Luke. He's quoting from prophecy in the book of Isaiah. Jesus brought good news. He healed the blind, set people free from sin's bondage, and proclaimed victory.

What victory has God accomplished in your life?

Where have you seen renewal even in the past few weeks?

What is God challenging you to do next?

My prayer to God today is:

_____

_____

_____

_____

_____

_____

_____

Hope in Action

THE FOLLOWING PRAYER IS FROM JOHN 17, Jesus's prayer right before he was arrested. He prayed for his disciples, but he prayed for you and me too. Where you see the brackets added below, insert your first name. Then, read through this prayer of Jesus.

After saying all these things, Jesus looked up to heaven and said, "Father, the hour has come. Glorify your Son so he can give glory back to you. For you have given him authority over everyone. He gives eternal life to each one you have given him. And this is the way to have eternal life—to know you, the only true God, and Jesus Christ, the one you sent to earth. I brought glory to you here on earth by completing the work you gave me to do. Now, Father, bring me into the glory we shared before the world began.

"I have revealed you to the ones you gave me from this world. They were always yours. You gave them to me, and they have kept your word. Now they know that everything I have is a gift from you, for I have passed on to them the message you gave me. They accepted it and know that I came from you, and they believe you sent me.

"My prayer is not for the world, but for those you have given me, because they belong to you. All who are mine belong to you, and you have given them to me, so they bring me glory. Now I am departing from the world; they are staying in this world, but I am coming to you. Holy Father, you have given me your name; now protect them by the power of your name so that they will be united just as we are. During my time here, I protected them by the power of the name you gave me. I guarded them so that not one was lost, except the one headed for destruction, as the Scriptures foretold.

"Now I am coming to you. I told them many things while I was with them in this world so they would be filled with my joy. I have given them your word. And the world hates them because they do not belong to the world, just as I do not belong to the world. I'm not asking you to take them out of the world, but to keep them safe from the evil one. They do not belong to this world any more than I do. Make them holy by your truth; teach them your word, which is truth. Just as you sent me into the world, I am sending them into the world. And I give myself as a holy sacrifice for them so they can be made holy by your truth.

"I am praying not only for these disciples but also for all who will ever believe in me through their message. I pray that they will all be one, just as you and I are one—as you are in me, Father, and I am in you. And may [_____] be in us so that the world will believe you sent me.

"I have given [_____] the glory you gave me, so [_____] may be one as we are one. I am in them and you are in me. May [_____] experience such perfect unity that the world will know that you sent me and that you love [_____] as much as you love me. Father, I want these whom you have given me to be with me where I am. Then they can see all the glory you gave me because you loved me even before the world began!

"O righteous Father, the world doesn't know you, but I do; and these disciples know you sent me. I have revealed you to [_____], and I will continue to do so. Then your love for me will be in [_____], and I will be in [_____]."

Make a plan to put Jesus's love into forward action to embody his love and commitment to someone else. Look for an impactful thing you can do to serve someone else. It might be delivering a care package or helping with a project. Making a meal or babysitting for an afternoon. Driving someone to an appointment or keeping them company. Look for a need you can meet that will bless and encourage someone else.

WRITE YOUR PLAN HERE:

_____

_____

_____

_____

_____

_____

_____

_____

_____

_____

_____

_____

After you test it out, add a date and reminder to your calendar for when you'll try your next loving service act.

Bonus Meditations

WE COVERED SO MUCH OF THE BOOK of John here. The part that follows what you studied in *Renewed* includes the account of Jesus's arrest, trial, crucifixion, death, and resurrection. I didn't skip over that part to minimize what is the most important event in history. This book prepares you to see Jesus's death and resurrection in a new way.

I invite you to use the following one-week reading plan to meditate and reflect on how this applies to you personally. Consider each of the themes from this book as you read: refill, receive, replenish, reclaim, rebirth, and remain. You may wish to use this reading plan for your own personal retreat time, the Hope in Action step in chapter 2.

Seven Meditations on Jesus's Death and Resurrection

READING 1: JOHN 18:1-14

Focus: Jesus's arrest in Gethsemane and his initial court hearing before Annas.

Reflection: Consider Jesus's willingness to be arrested and how his submission to the Father's will refreshes our understanding of obedience. Reflect on how abiding in Jesus, even in difficult times, can lead to spiritual strength and peace.

_____

_____

_____

_____

_____

READING 2: JOHN 18:1-27

Focus: Peter's denial of Jesus and Jesus's questioning by the high priest.

Reflection: Reflect on Peter's fear and denial, and how Jesus remained composed under questioning. Consider how returning to Jesus after failing refreshes our spirit and re-establishes our connection to his love.

_____

_____

_____

_____

_____

READING 3: JOHN 18:28-40

Focus: Jesus's trial before Pilate and the crowd choosing Barabbas over Jesus.

Reflection: Think about Pilate's struggle between justice and public pressure. Reflect on how Jesus's commitment to his mission refreshes our faith and demonstrates the depth of his love. Abiding in him helps us stand firm in our convictions.

_____

_____

_____

_____

_____

READING 4: JOHN 19:1-16

Focus: Jesus's sentencing, mocking, and Pilate presenting Jesus to the crowd.

Reflection: Meditate on the suffering Jesus endured and how his steadfastness refreshes our understanding of sacrificial love. Abiding in Jesus gives us the strength to endure trials and reflect his love to others.

_____

_____

_____

_____

_____

READING 5: JOHN 19:17-42

Focus: The crucifixion, death, and burial of Jesus.

Reflection: Contemplate the significance of Jesus's sacrifice and his final words. Reflecting Jesus's sacrificial love is essential for producing the spiritual fruit of love in our lives.

_____

_____

_____

_____

_____

READING 6: JOHN 20:1-18

Focus: The empty tomb and Jesus's appearance to Mary Magdalene.

Reflection: Reflect on the joy and astonishment of the resurrection. Consider how the resurrection renews our hope and empowers us to abide in Jesus, resulting in the fruit of love and joy.

_____

_____

_____

_____

_____

_____

READING 7: JOHN 20:19-21:25

Focus: Jesus's appearances to his disciples, including Thomas, and the final appearance by the Sea of Galilee.

Reflection: Reflect on the importance of faith and Jesus's reinstatement of Peter. Abiding in Jesus helps us produce the fruit of love. Contemplate how Jesus's continual presence and instruction refreshes our spirit and guides us in loving others.

_____

_____

_____

_____

_____

Jesus, help me to abide in you and find my refreshment and strength in you. I invite your sacrificial love to replenish my spirit and transform my heart. As I reflect on these passages, fill me with a renewed sense of purpose and a deeper connection to your love. Grant me the courage to live out these truths, bearing the fruit of love in my daily life. May your Spirit lead, refresh, and empower me to share your love with those around me. Amen.

LOOK FOR OTHER BOOKS IN THE REMADE SERIES:

Acknowledgments

I'M GRATEFUL TO JESUS FOR BEING PATIENT with me as I sort through my understanding of so much of my childhood faith. He has truly continued the work he started in me as a child and has never left—even when I ask a lot of questions.

My grandfather taught me a lot about life and gardening. He's with the Master Gardener now, but I can still hear him say, "Honey," right before a gardening tip or life lesson ensued.

Kathy Carlton Willis, I've said it before, and it bears repeating. I appreciate the industry chats, but even more, your friendship. Thank you for being a safe confidant as I wrestle through God's repurposing and renewing. It isn't as lonely when someone has your back!

Robyn Mulder, you are a meticulous editor and a wonderful writer. Thank you for putting your skills to work here.

I know there are many people to thank. But I'm all out of words. Poured them all out and wrestled with the concepts. Reader, if there is one thing that kept me going when words and thoughts felt jumbled, it was you. More than anything, I want this to be a resource that helps you discover the fruit of abiding in Jesus. Love really is the most wonderful thing. Thank you for trusting me with your Bible study time.

> I pray that from his glorious, unlimited resources he will empower you with inner strength through his Spirit. Then Christ will make his home in your hearts as you trust in him. Your roots will grow down into God's love and keep you strong. And may you have the power to understand, as all God's people should, how wide, how long, how high, and how deep his love is. May you experience the love of Christ, though it is too great to understand fully. Then you will be made complete with all the fullness of life and power that comes from God.
>
> —Ephesians 3:16–19

A free printable 8x10 art image inspired by
this book series is waiting for you at

WWW.MICHELLERAYBURN.COM/REMADE

If you've enjoyed this book, please write a review
on your favorite bookstore platform and help
spread the word about the series. Thank you!

About the Author

MICHELLE RAYBURN DELIGHTS IN REPURPOSED JUNK, GREAT books, dark chocolate, and iced coffee—and summer Sunday afternoons in the hammock with the latter three. As a writer and podcast host, she helps others discover the joy of finding hope in the trashy stuff of life. The *Midlife Repurposed* podcast and Substack blog feature humorous life observations, tools for spiritual growth, and inspirational stories of hope.

Among Michelle's books are *Classic Marriage* (winner of a Golden Scroll Award, Christian Market Book Award, and finalist in Next Gen Indie Book Awards), *The Repurposed and Upcycled Life* (Write-to-Publish Writer of the Year award), and *Life, Repurposed* (Golden Scroll Award honorable mention). *Renewed*, the first book in the REMADE Bible study series was a 2024 Selah Awards Finalist.

Michelle has a master's in ministry leadership with a pastoral counseling emphasis. She enjoys speaking for women's events where she can blend Bible teaching with humor and wisdom from life's imperfect moments.

She and her high school sweetheart, Phil, have been fine-tuning their classic marriage for more than three decades. They've raised two boys, and the family tree has branched to include two daughters-in-law and four grandchildren (and counting). They make their home in the Northwoods of Wisconsin in a century-old former church and parsonage.

www.michellerayburn.com

www.ingramcontent.com/pod-product-compliance
Lightning Source LLC
Chambersburg PA
CBHW080755120626
46557CB00006B/1277